THANK GOD IT'S MONDAY!

14 Values We Need to Humanize the Way We Work

THANK GOD IT'S MONDAY!

14 Values We Need to Humanize the Way We Work

Kenneth Cloke and Joan Goldsmith

IRWIN
Professional Publishing®

Chicago • London • Singapore

This publication is designed to provide accurate and
authoritative information in regard to the subject matter
covered. It is sold with the understanding that neither the
author or the publisher is engaged in rendering legal, accounting,
or other professional service. If legal advice or other expert
assistance is required, the services of a competent professional
person should be sought.

*From a Declaration of Principles jointly adopted by a Committee
of the American Bar Association and a Committee of Publishers.*

**Times Mirror
Higher Education Group**

Library of Congress Cataloging-in-Publication Data
Cloke, Ken (date)
    Thank God It's Monday! : 14 values we need to humanize the way we
work/by Kenneth Cloke and Joan Goldsmith
        p.   cm.
    Includes index.
    ISBN 0-7863-1096-0
    I. Quality of work life. 2. Work environment. 3. Organizational
change. 4. Management. I. Goldsmith, Joan. II. Title
HD6955.C56 1997   96–31794
658.3′14—dc20

Printed in the United States of America
1 2 3 4 5 6 7 8 9 0 3 2 I 0 9 8 7 6

To those with whom we have worked,
who have been our teachers;

to Joan's former father-in-law, Douglas McGregor,
who was among the first to point the way;

to our friend Warren Bennis,
who led us to our own truth;

to our mothers and fathers,
who through love turned drudgery into joyful work;

and to our children, nieces, nephews, and siblings,
who inspired us to write this book,
that their work lives may be sources
of learning, growth, and love.

CONTENTS

THREE

UNDERSTANDING HOW WE GOT HERE   43

FOUR

HOW WE CAN HUMANIZE THE WAY WE WORK   61

FIVE

REINVENTING THE WHEEL   89

SIX

EMBRACING CHANGE 115

SEVEN

SEEING CONFLICT AS OPPORTUNITY 159

EIGHT

WHY HUMANIZE THE WAY WE WORK?   207

It is highly likely that in the next decade the United States will experience a period of social unrest unequaled in this century. It will dwarf the protests of the late 1960s and early 1970s. The strikes and demonstrations that occurred recently in France are a portent of what may lie in the future for us. A number of trends have lead me to this dreary prediction:

- **The growing disparity between the nation's rich and poor.** In the middle of the 1970s, the income gap between the very rich and the very poor was at its narrowest: 1 percent of the population controlled 18 percent of private wealth; now, 1 percent of the population controls 40 percent of the wealth.

  Corporations reflect the same widening gap between the haves and have-nots. There is a colossal disparity between the average pay of CEOs and the pay of the average worker; estimates of the ratio range up to 140 to 1. The disparity persists even in adverse times. While CEOs walk away from mergers and other corporate upheavals with multimillion dollar golden parachutes, the downsized thousands get a few months severance pay and lose sleep over their loss of healthcare coverage.

- **The abandonment of the "other half."** British management philosopher Charles Handy wrote about a CEO who boasted that his equation for success was "half times two times three equals success." The CEO explained that with half the workforce he could produce twice as many goods with three times the revenues. Not bad. But, Handy asks, "What about the other half?" Most of us try to duck the question or finesse it. Some business leaders respond by talking about "employability." They say that they cannot guarantee job security, but can provide knowledge and tools for their laid-off workers to find employment elsewhere. But where is the "elsewhere" these days? And who knows just what knowledge and tools are going to work the necessary magic in a shrinking job market?

- **The inversion of trust.** In the mid-1950s, about 70 percent of Americans believed our government was genuinely concerned with the common good. Trust in government began to erode noisily in the mid-1960s and continues to decline at an accelerating rate. Recent studies indicate that only 25 percent of Americans now trust their government. Vice President Al Gore tells the apocryphal story of a government pollster who asked: "Do you trust the government more or less than you did five years ago?" Ten percent of those surveyed said they trusted the government more; 15 percent said they trusted it less; the remaining 75 percent refused to answer—they thought the survey was some sort of government plot.

- **The lack of genuine empowerment.** Even those who are still employed work in a chronic state of anxiety. For them, empowerment is an increasingly Orwellian term, not simply a lie, but an infuriating inversion of the truth. A demoralizing sense of powerlessness is what many jobholders are feeling. Nearly everyone worries about getting a pink slip or avoids taking risks for fear of getting one.

When I use the word *empowerment*, I refer, for example, to Jan Carlzon, the leader who transformed SAS, changed the way we think about airlines, and truly embodies empowerment. He tells us that genuine empowerment means:

> *To free someone from rigorous control by instructions, policies, and orders, and to give that person freedom to take responsibility for his ideas, decisions, and actions . . . to release hidden resources that would otherwise remain inaccessible to both the individual and an organization.*

How is it possible to create empowered workplaces in the absence of trust? And why should any employee trust management under the conditions outlined above? The kind of trust that is necessary for truly creative, risk-taking work has become a nostalgic memory.

These problems have grown worse as a result of the recent trend toward reengineering, which in the eyes of employees means "downsizing" and a lack of respect for years of service. Empowerment and reengineering are now on a collision course. It's impossible for a company to reengineer, downsize, and empower at the same time, though many firms are attempting it.

Unless the private sector finds a way to both make money and reestablish a sense of trust in the workplace, we will continue to be in trouble. Worried workers do not engage in the kind of creative problem solving that contemporary businesses require. And unless some solution is found to the dilemma facing those who are losing their jobs—a population segment that now includes the middle class as well as the poor—we will see public expressions of rage and fear that will make the recent strikes in France look like a stroll in the park.

This book by Ken Cloke and Joan Goldsmith is a highly useful tool in the effort to respond to these problems. It is essential for any organization that is seeking to transform and prevail over the traumas of our times to redirect its energies back to its employees and make them the drivers of transformation and the builders of productive new environments. What follows in this book are the stories and the wisdom Ken and Joan have gathered as they have assisted so many of us to empower ourselves and one another in our efforts to transform the way we work.

We need this book to redirect ourselves back to the human values that should form the core of our organizations. And we need empowering leaders to provide guidance and create the models we need in this new effort.

As many of you know, I have long been absorbed with the issue of leadership and coauthored a book on leadership with Joan Goldsmith. The kind of empowering leadership that Cloke and Goldsmith call for can be generated at any point in our lives or in those of our organizations.

I have been thinking recently about the leadership exhibited by Winston Churchill, who really didn't achieve greatness until he was 66 years old. It was said about Churchill in one of his biographies that he jaywalked his way through life. Or there is Bertrand Russell, who as he got older, took greater risks in writing about philosophy; or Mel Torme, who keeps singing publicly at the age of 70 and keeps cresting, never coasting. These people didn't stop; they kept on going, and we need to think about what allowed them to do so.

What is true of all these people, and of most of the successful executives I've known, is that at some point in their lives, they stopped trying to prove themselves and began to express themselves. That transition is a very interesting one, one I'm not sure I've accomplished myself.

Bill Bradley, the senator from New Jersey, is an excellent example of this kind of leadership. It wasn't until he was almost defeated by Christine Todd Whitman in 1992 that he began to think about what he was doing in politics. He began to realize that he was beginning to shade his speeches ever so subtly to please a particular audience. It wasn't that he consciously lied or was deceitful. But he found ways to spin his remarks so that they would please others; to seek approval without really expressing himself. He said it reminded him of when he played basketball at Princeton where he had been a major college star. He said, "Even then, when I was playing for the fans, I wasn't nearly as effective a player as when I was playing to do the best I could for the team."

It seems to me there is a profound difference between having to prove yourself and having the capacity to express yourself, and that difference is the central topic and focus of this book. I think this book can empower you to make a difference in your work life. It can enable you to express yourself through your work and not just prove yourself to your boss. For the past 30 years, my life has been committed to finding ways of enabling myself, my students, clients, family, and friends to be more truly themselves and express more of who they are in the daily process of life. We have a valuable guide for just such an endeavor in this book. Use it well. You will be able to be more yourself as a result.

Warren Bennis
University of Southern California

The Human Side of Change

If you have ever tried to change a habit, you know how difficult change can be. Imagine the complexity when we try to change an entire organization, with its complex rules, cultures, and systems. It is relatively easy to alter the language we use to describe what we have always done, so that instead of serving on *committees* we now serve on *teams*. It is much more difficult to change our *behaviors*, the ways we think and act, and especially the ways we work. A committee is not the same as a team, even if we put a different label on it, and making it into a genuine team takes enormous effort.

The most difficult part of the change process for all of us, and the element most likely to be overlooked in organizations, whether they are corporations, schools, government agencies, or nonprofits, is the *human* side of the enterprise. Our corporations, government agencies, and nonprofit organizations are all going through rapid change, but few are measuring the human costs and benefits in the process.

Many of our organizations are rapidly engaged in revamping their strategies, changing their structures, reengineering their systems, and downsizing to become more efficient or profitable, then hoping their employees will go along with the proposed changes. They assume employees who were not involved in deciding on these changes and don't understand what they mean will buy in and figure out on their own what they are supposed to do after the decisions have already been made. Unfortunately, it doesn't work that way in practice.

An example of what we mean comes from one of the largest aerospace corporations in the country. After spending more than $1,500,000 and 14 months into a CEO-mandated change process, we were asked to help align the top 50 executives behind a reengineering process that they had been sabotaging. When we arrived, the top executives had decided to implement new work process teams, an aggressive customer service campaign, and "decision gates" to monitor their decision-making process, and there was a great deal of lip service, or public compliance, at the top.

But behind the scenes, public compliance had turned into private defiance, and the teams were being met with apathy, resistance, and sabotage from the managers who were supposed to make it work. These problems could have been averted if alignment had begun two years earlier by involving managers and employees in the planning process. Now upper management was faced with backtracking, listening to objections, correcting their course, and replanning the implementation, all because the leaders had not considered the needs of the human beings who felt they were being manipulated like robots in the change process.

When we speak to organizational leaders and people on the front lines of the change process, we hear the same complaints. As one of the employees we spoke with said:

> We've been through many change processes. We've tried reengineering, we've redesigned our work processes, we've restructured, we constantly have a new plan, which we call the 'flavor of the month,' but we can't seem to break through to behave differently.

There is widespread cynicism in many of the organizations we work with about the change process, mostly as a result of change efforts that treat employees inhumanely or insensitively; that ignore the input they give; that do not seek their wisdom, advice, or participation; that do not see them as active partners in the process; that do not reach the real problems; and that are uncritical of the process used to design and implement the change. Change efforts of this kind result only in cynicism, depression, and apathy; in public compliance that masks private defiance; and in outright resistance and sabotage.

> US. corporations will spend over 34 billion dollars on reengineering in the coming year and three-fourths of the projects will fail because the people issues are not addressed.
>
> Mike Hammer

We have organized our workplaces to improve their efficiency and bottom-line profitability, but we have not thought carefully enough about organizing them to satisfy human needs as well. Three employees in the entertainment industry describe the pressures of their current work realities this way:

> I can't get it all done. I could live here and not get it all done. I struggle with am I good enough. The hours are killers and I wonder how I will stay afloat with all the demands. I churn in the night with the problems. I never feel I'm off the job.

I don't think we have successfully addressed the quality-of-life issues. We pay lip service, but ultimately there is a pressure to produce that requires everything possible within the bounds of human limitation.

What do they think of us, are we chopped chicken liver? When do we get the skills, the funds, or the support?

And it's not just the corporate world that ignores the human factor. A recent large-scale school reform effort began by sending the principal and union chairperson from dozens of schools to a month of management training at a cost of more than $30,000 per pair. The tens of thousands of teachers, administrators, staff, and parents who were left behind without resources to implement the change effort asked us why that money could not have been used to train them instead. The pair who receive the training will need it—if only to overcome the negative responses and false expectations that will greet them when they return.

Transforming the Work Environment

Why is the human side of the change process the last element that is thought out, the forgotten part of the plan, the piece of the puzzle that always seems to get lost on the floor? Why don't we begin the work of designing our organizations with ourselves and the needs of our co-workers in mind? Is it too threatening, too difficult, too overwhelming? Usually we expect that people's human needs will take care of themselves, or we hope they will go away. But it never works that way.

The change process illustrates most dramatically the costs of ignoring the needs of employees. However, the entire work process, down to the ways we act and interact with each other at work, has to be conceived in human terms. We often fail to treat each other with courtesy or respect; we allow problems to develop simply because they do not fit directly under our assigned roles; we place decision making far from the practical expertise that is needed for it to succeed; we punish those who point out what isn't working; and then we wonder why so many people have negative attitudes about their work lives and are unable to achieve their full potential!

The costs of ignoring employees also extends to the profitability of the business. How much time and energy in your workplace is spent on gossip and rumors? How much time and energy is spent on unresolved conflicts? On miscommunication? On overcoming resistance to change? On lawsuits and complaints? If we start adding up the time spent in these largely unnecessary pursuits, the total cost of not treating people as adults is enormous!

These costs also extend to society. In the five years between 1991 and 1996, we lost nearly 3,000,000 jobs to downsizing. Many of those who lost their jobs were unable to find new ones or replace them with jobs that paid as well. Many lost their health insurance policies and pensions, and many became embittered and angry as a result of the way they were treated. These injuries have had an impact on our society and our political life in ways we do not yet fully realize.

In our experience we have found that it is possible to organize work differently. It is possible to satisfy human needs, to take pleasure in our work, to create organizations that encourage and support each individual's contribution, to treat one another respectfully, and to increase productivity at the same time. We have discovered that to achieve these ends, we had to identify the core values and processes that help us change the way we work and then begin to systematically rethink all of our work processes from that standpoint. This book will show you what it will take to create a workplace that is both pleasurable and productive.

Why We Wrote This Book

For the past 30 years, we have been focusing on the human side of change. Some of our clients have called us "change junkies" because we love observing, impacting, and learning about the change process. We are revitalized when we watch our colleagues grow and expand with their involvement in the change process. We like being around people who are struggling with the personal and organizational problems and conflicts that grow out of being open to change, which makes them more interesting, full of energy and life, and willing to grapple with problems that are worth solving.

Our own experiences with change began in the upheavals and transformations of the 1960s and 70s. We learned a great deal that appears in these pages from the social change movements of that period and from our experiences in political organizing, law, teaching, family therapy, historical research, arbitration, education, judging, mediation, and conflict resolution. We also learned a great deal about change by studying political theory, educational reform, community empowerment, social history, psychology, and spiritual and ecological thinking. And we have learned by being employees and managers ourselves.

Today, we work with many individuals and organizations conducting trainings and workshops on team building, strategic planning, conflict resolution, prejudice reduction, collaborative negotiation, and other topics that focus on changing the way we work. We work as mediators resolving a wide variety of personal and organizational disputes. We interview, assess, envision, design, consult, facilitate, train, coach, investigate, encourage dialogue, plan, and evaluate. And, like the rest of you, we are learning as we go.

While each of our experiences has been unique, we have learned similar lessons from all of them: lessons about including everyone in the process; about communicating respectfully and honestly; about collaborating and smoothing the way; about taking risks and being creative; about leading empathically and courageously; about facing our conflicts directly rather than avoiding them; and about the need to acknowledge and support the humanity and celebrate the diversity of each person. This book is an effort to summarize what we've learned from these experiences, the triumphs as well as the mistakes, what was successful and what was not, because this is part of what it means to be human.

Our purpose in this book is to identify the strategies and solutions that public- and private-sector organizations have used to bring about a different kind of workplace, and to do so through a different kind of change process, one that leads to participation, enthusiasm, involvement, and ownership.

Our Audience

We have written this book for those of you who have been catapulted into the change process without being asked for your opinion or knowing how to find your bearings. We have written it for internal and external consultants, change agents, and reengineering "experts" who have not been given adequate support or training; for organizational leaders who are wondering where and how they are leading; for those who are struggling to make sense of the direction being taken in organizational change; and for those, perhaps including yourself, who are dissatisfied with the way their workplace is organized, or find their work unpleasurable because it does not acknowledge or satisfy their personal needs.

We have also written this book for those who are wondering about the direction of postindustrial or postmodern society, and for those who are worrying about the impact the current change process is having on our lives. What will be the result of all the layoffs and downsizing we are experiencing? How can we organize our work so as to counteract the stresses and meet the challenges that flow from increasing competition, reengineering scarce resources, time pressures, population growth, decline of government funding, consumer demands, ecological deterioration, increased cultural and ethnic diversity, and the lack of a clear vision of where we are heading and why? All of these issues generate organizational, interpersonal, and social conflicts which we can no longer ignore. And they all indicate possibilities for future growth and learning which we can no longer do without.

We hope this book will be useful not only for corporations, but also for organizations such as schools trying to survive and improve the way they teach, for children's service agencies undergoing downsizing and the elimination of programs, and for nonprofits trying to meet the needs of a changing population while facing professional burnout.

Many of us imagine that our public institutions are in tune with the needs of their staffs, but that is not often the case in service organizations. With the onslaught of federal block grants and cuts in services, increased pressures from clients and customers, and the lack of an empathetic and empowering leadership, the very people who should be helping others aren't getting the help they need to do so, and are often in need of help themselves.

Consider our recent experience working with the district office of a large federal agency in which employees had nowhere to go with problems or complaints if they were not covered in the collective bargaining agreement. In this agency, if issues were not definable as grievances that could be addressed by the formal procedures dictated by the labor contract, they were ignored by management and allowed to fester.

In another example, an up-and-coming regional healthcare provider began a several-million-dollar reengineering project designed to convert it into a sleek competitor in a fiercely competitive market. We discovered that the leaders of the change effort were confused about its direction when the head of medical services and the chief of the insurance section asked, "What business are we actually in?" and no one was able to give an answer. We proposed that the reengineering process be halted until that question was answered. Their response was, "We'll get to that issue later." But later is too late. If the leaders don't know what direction they are taking or what their mission is, how can anyone else be expected to follow?

In each of these examples, conflicts were created by ignoring the questions, opinions, and concerns of the people whose support was required to make the organization successful. The cost of these conflicts to the organizations involved was and is immense, in wasted time, money, effort, and morale. There is a better way.

A New Work Environment

We offer the lessons we have learned from our clients about changing the contexts and paradigms of our work, about how we can go about rethinking the way we work, about the core elements of what makes a workplace "human," about what makes change successful, and about a collaborative approach to resolving conflicts. Most of all, this book is an action guide directed at what can be done, starting tomorrow. Our purpose is to provide you with information, creative ideas, and practical activities that will enable you to create a work environment that draws everyone in, that inspires everyone, that gives everyone a sense of freedom and satisfaction, and that allows all our talents to flower through all the stages of our work lives and careers. We know from our own experiences that work can be a way for us to feel we are contributing to a greater good, and that we are doing so without sacrificing our own needs for personal growth and challenge, social interaction, mental and physical health, emotional support, spiritual expression, and active participation in the decisions that affect our lives.

The voices of our many clients, friends, and colleagues who have worked long and hard to create these kinds of organizations tell us that this is so. Here are some of their words expressing the excitement that becomes possible when the human side of work is acknowledged and supported:

I have stopped complaining and started doing.
I am now able to look at my job in a totally different light.
I'm paying more attention to process, not just product—and it's paying off.
It feels good to express myself more (with less fear of reprisal).

I'm doing less and more: I defer less and communicate more.
I've learned to question more, especially the traditional rules and processes.
I can be more creative.
I've developed personally. I can be more open, assertive, and take the initiative.
I've finally found out how and where I fit in!

Acknowledgments

Like the winners of Academy Awards, we have many people to thank for what appears in these pages and too little space to do it in. First, we would like to acknowledge the helpful comments and support we received from our families and friends, from Dick, Shirley, Bill, Angie, Kristin, Elka and Nick Cloke; Miriam, Steve, Gretel, and Sam Goldsmith; Shetu Nandy and Tinku Ray; Sidney and Yulin Rittenberg; Beth Farb; Joan MacIntosh; Monte and Betty Factor; John, Cathy, Emily and Chloe Schaefer, Marcia Schiff, and Ron O'Connor.

We also want to acknowledge the real-life visionary leaders with whom we have talked and worked, who live the principles we are describing, and from whom we have learned much that is contained in these pages. These include Warren Bennis, Grace Gabe, Blenda Wilson, Louis Fair, Peggy Dulany, Roberto Mizrahi, Bruce Schearer, Elahe Hessemfar, Susan Evans, Peter Clarke, Ian and Donna Mitroff, Dick Beckhart, George Rusznak, Eileen Brown, Reno James, Gil Dube, Ellen Dempsey, Lucia Diaz, Elaine Brown, Gustavo and Nicole Esteva, Nancy Hollander, Steve Portugese, Marvin and Cathy Treiger, Bill Gallegos, Joan Dunlop, Peter and Hope Schneider, Tom Schumacher, Tim Engel, Faith Raiguel, Jimmy Loyce, Lance Dublin, Steve Heffernan, Michael Johnston, Ann Overton, Susaan Straus, Mariella Colombe, Angel Luis Portoundo, Oneida Alvarez, Arturo Rodriguez, Oscar Aramos, Maria-Antonia Rodriguez, Eduardo Cruz, Helen Bernstein, Adam Urbanski, Ann Cook, Marcella Howell, Edgar Hayes, Tom Hayden, Noreen Clark, Sithembiso Nyoni, Graca Machel, Thongbai Thongpao, Bill Jersey, John Mack, Robin Kramer, Peggy Funkhauser, Rajesh Tandon, Ashis Nandy, Wanda Angel Aduan, and many others too numerous to mention.

We especially want to thank our editor, Caroline Carney, who sharpened and polished the text with intelligent and loving care. And many thanks to Mike Cohn who believed in this book and made it happen.

ONE

We Are What We Do

One's philosophy is not best expressed in words, it is expressed in the choices one makes. In the long run, we shape our lives and we shape ourselves. The process never ends until we die. And the choices we make are ultimately our responsibility.

ELEANOR ROOSEVELT

$\mathbf{T}$hink of your own job. How much of yourself do you bring to what you do, and how much do you tuck away or save until work is over?

To understand better what we mean when we refer to creating a work environment that embraces human characteristics, we first need to take a look at who we really are and see ourselves not simply as being, but as *becoming*, as works in progress who are constantly being shaped and recreated through our interactions with our surroundings and with others. We need to become more aware of how we actually feel, think, and act at work, and of the ways our feelings, thoughts, and actions give meaning to the rest of our lives.

What It Means to Create Ourselves through Our Work

One of the hidden truths of our work lives is that we manufacture not only cars and clothes, but *ourselves* through our work. We produce products, money, and services at work, but in the process, we also act, think, relate, and generate feelings, ideas, and emotions, and these experiences become a part of who we are. Each time we make a choice on the job, we shape our identities, our inner feelings about who we are, our sense of self-worth, and our relationships with others. Work gives us unlimited opportunities to develop our full potential. Yet for most of us, work is something we try to avoid or shun, and we envy those who are on vacation, retired or independently wealthy.

Over the course of our work lives, we spend more time with co-workers, customers and strangers than we do with our families and loved ones. Yet we spend almost *none* of our time at work considering how we might make it more pleasurable, more fulfilling, more expressive of who we really are. Efficiency, status, and bottom-line profits drive our workplace dynamics to such an extent that we've missed seeing that our work produces internal as well as external results. When the results are painful we find ourselves speaking tragically, as this employee did:

The biggest obstacle is the way we treat people. It is too difficult to make the sacrifices, including working on Mother's Day, Father's Day and my wife's birthday, and then not feel respected or acknowledged for what I have done. The pressure is always to deliver—what have you done for me today. I'm lost as a person, to my friends, to my family, to my life.

The double bind is that while empty or negative experiences at work often leave us wishing we were somewhere else, most of the creativity and challenge in our lives occurs at work. We can find that creativity and challenge in the production of cars or movies or books or service to others, but we can also find it in the choices we make about how we deliver those products. The way we work; the nature of our work relationships; how we respond to anger, criticism, conflict, challenge, success, and failure; help define our character. Work is not simply a means of achieving financial success, economic survival, personal status, or an excellent product; it is also potentially a means of *self-creation*, and therefore an end in itself.

We have been fortunate to work with many people over the years who have created themselves through their work. We saw a corporate accountant become a team leader, a receptionist become a trainer, and an engineer take on a human resource role, leaving his corporate position to become the senior manager of a social service agency. By becoming aware of who they were, what opportunities were available to them, and what they wanted in their lives, and through their commitment and the nurturing of their talent, these people found meaning in their work and became leaders in their own lives.

We have marveled at how a former housewife and Junior Leaguer with no experience in the job market transformed herself into the president of a multimillion dollar educational reform organization, and successfully led a large urban school reform initiative. We watched as she developed confidence, acquired new skills, and grew in professionalism. We have seen the manager of an information systems organization take the risk of leaving line management to become a corporate consultant and then return as chief information officer for a Fortune 100 corporation. We have cheered over the years as an administrative assistant to a corporate CEO became a senior vice president of a major organizational consulting firm and then moved on to start her own successful consulting and brokering business. We coached an insurance executive as he traded his corporate suit for overalls and a shovel and left behind a stress-filled vice presidency to start his own gardening and landscaping firm. In fact, we were one of his first clients. And we watched a receptionist who volunteered to coordinate a team-training event became a trainer herself and was promoted into a top-management position.

What these stories have in common is a capacity all of us share: the ability to learn and grow, to reinvent ourselves through what we do and how we do it. Work can be defined, simply, as a relationship between ourselves and productive activity. Unfortunately, it is often boring, bureaucratic, alienating, stressful, demeaning, and idiotic. But it can also be exciting, useful, healing, enjoyable, empowering, and creative. The difference between these alternatives lies in how we structure the work process, and how we *think* about the way we work.

If, as individuals or as organizations, we structure our work lives only to produce efficiency and profits, we will produce alienation and resistance as well. But if we create space in our work schedules for learning and enjoyment, if we put flowers in our factories and laughter in our offices, if we do not crush the human spirit with drudgery but let it sing, we will profit personally and outproduce any command and control based system.

For example, we worked with a large nationally known company to help reorganize its workforce into high-performance, self-directed teams. The company was motivated by a desire to increase productivity and profitability, which it achieved, but working in a team environment also helped the individual team members grow, which increased their enjoyment of work. Members of one of these self-directed teams made the following statements:

"For the first time in my life, I'm meeting my potential."

"I can now empower myself to fix my own problems."

"I find myself working smarter."

"It is thrilling to be able to stretch my beliefs, concepts, and abilities."

How Our Activities and Choices Create Us: An Exercise

Take a minute to step back from the day-to-day pressures of your job. This exercise is an opportunity to conduct a quick analysis of how you spend your time at work and how your work impacts the way you think of yourself. Complete the chart below based on what you did in the past week; use extra paper if necessary.

Notice what your actual activities and choices are at work. Don't pick only the major decisions, such as whether you competed for a promotion; pick the small ones as well, such as how often you acknowledged your co-workers. And don't pick only those that triggered positive feelings; also pick the ones that left you feeling drained or angry. How did each of these activities contribute to your personal growth and to what defines the organization? What was the impact of these activities on your sense of who you are, on your identity?

Activity or Choice	Contribution to Personal Growth	Contribution to Organization
1.		
2.		
3.		
4.		
5.		

Share your results with someone you trust, whether a member of your family, a friend, partner, spouse, or co-worker on the job. Ask that person to reflect on how these decisions contributed to you or your organization, or the impact they had on your personal development. If other members of your organization have completed this chart, share with them and compare your responses with theirs. Do you see a pattern in your contributions or the way your activities impact your personal growth? Does your organization encourage you to take the initiative and make contributions based on individual choices? If not, can you find a way to motivate your organization to open the possibilities for greater freedom to contribute to the work process? What other changes could you make in your work activities to improve yourself and your organization?

Envisioning the Future of Work

In order to become more strategic about our futures we need to become more conscious of the limiting influence outdated ideas have on our imagination. The primary constraints in our lives arise from the way we think, particularly about work, change, and conflict. Our attitudes and approaches to these experiences help to determine whether what we create is positive or negative, whether it results in growth or resistance.

Once we have seen the impact our work has on our personal development, we can start to think about how we might change the work process to support our growth and learning. The first step in this process is to escape the gravitational pull into what we already know. We have found envisioning a very powerful technique for guiding organizations and individuals toward positive change.

A vision is a statement about what you or your organization will look like in the future. It is inspirational yet clear, challenging yet sensible, stable yet flexible, and prepares for the future while honoring the past. It is lived in the details of its execution. A vision:

- Engages our hearts and spirits.
- Taps into embedded concerns and needs.
- Is an assertion of what we and our colleagues want to create.
- Is something worth striving for.
- Provides meaning to the work people do in the organization.
- Is a little cloudy and grand.
- Is simple and empowering.
- Describes not only outcomes but also processes.
- Is a living document that can always be added to.
- Is a starting place to reach greater levels of specificity.
- Is based on a deep human need for quality and dedication.
- Is not just about what you want to do or have, but also about what you want to be.

The future is created out of the choices we make moment by moment in the present, yet we make these choices for the most part without a sense of long-range direction. Many of the goals or outcomes we pursue require years of cumulative action and visions are a way of giving form and purpose to those actions. Visions help establish a basis of consensus within which everyone can belong; they create a sense of ownership, build teamwork, and improve our communication and relationships. They allow us to begin with what we agree on so our disagreements can be put in perspective.

How many of you have sat down with your co-workers to create a vision for how your future workplace might be organized? Have you stopped to consider all the possible ways of organizing your work before you begin to reengineer your work processes? Have you allowed yourself to dream creatively about what it could be like? Have you looked closely at the way you have structured your work, and at your attitudes and relationships with colleagues?

We know that the future workplace will differ dramatically from the present, as the factories of the industrial revolution differed from the work spaces of the feudal artisans that preceded it. William Bridges in his *Fortune Magazine* cover story heralding "The End of the Job," described four traits of organizations that make the traditional job, as a way of organizing work, a throwback to the past. The new "de-jobbed" environments will focus on the skills, talents, and interests of employees, matching them with the tasks to be done, the problems to be solved, and the results to be achieved. Bridges believes these new, futuristic organizations will behave as follows:

- They will encourage rank-and-file employees to make the kind of operating decisions previously reserved for managers.
- They will give people the information they need to make these decisions—information that used to be given only to managers.
- They will provide employees with training and at a CEO's level of business and financial knowledge.
- They will give everyone involved a stake in the fruits of their labor, a share not only in decision making but also in company profits.

We see many of these changes taking place now. Where they are heading and how we understand the direction in which they are taking us is the subject of this book. In later chapters we will explain more fully our vision for the new workplace and the new organization. Here is a chance for you to begin thinking about and envisioning your future.

The Future Is Now: An Exercise

For science-fiction buffs this exercise may be a piece of cybercake. We would like you to project yourself beyond the millennium to 15 or 20 years from now. Many of you will still be in the workforce. What do you think it will be like? How will work be accomplished? Here is one possible vision of the future workplace: There are no factories or fixed workplaces, no job titles, no job descriptions, no career paths, no bosses, no employees, no fixed responsibilities, no time clocks, no preset wages, and nothing is determined that cannot be changed. In other words, there are no jobs like the ones we know today.

In their place are small, diverse, decentralized, electronically linked, independent, mobile, electronically connected, democratic, hands-on, fast-forming, self-directed, self-managing, empowered project teams with rotating leaders, in which everyone is responsible for the entire effort, with wages based not only on time spent at the task but on productivity, team process, collaborative skills, continuing education, personal improvement, profitability, and customer satisfaction.

Take a few minutes to create your own future scenario. Do not begin with what is now in place, but let your mind wander and stretch. Answer the following questions about your work life, and if possible, share them with others. It will be helpful to you to communicate what you most want for the future with your co-workers, your boss, or your spouse or partner. How do their answers agree with yours? Where do you part company? What do you value the most? The feedback others give you can help you sharpen your vision.

1. Close your eyes and imagine the future place where you will work. What will it look like? Is it a building, a field, a house? Are you in a community center, an office or factory, a school of the future? What are the colors, the shapes, the sizes of the structures?

_____

_____

_____

2. What are you doing? Are you at a desk, on a telecommunications network, working on a computer, talking with a team, drawing charts and graphs? Are you teaching others?

_____

_____

_____

3. What is the feeling or tone? Are you laughing, serious, thoughtful, playful, focused, or scattered?

_____

_____

_____

4. Who is with you? Are you alone, writing or thinking? Are you with others solving problems? Are you in charge, taking orders, working with colleagues?

_____

_____

_____

5. What resources are available to you? Do you have desks, computers, electronic networks, telecommunications, videos, rapid transportation, computer-aided graphics, and instruction? What other resources are available?

_____

_____

_____

6. What skills will you need to be successful? How do you gain them? How will you expand and continue to learn? What interests and talents will you need and have?

_____

_____

_____

7. What is the focus of your work? How do you spend your time? What is the most important accomplishment you can picture?

_____

_____

_____

8. How do you feel about yourself in the new environment? How are you treated? How do you feel about your co-workers? How do you feel about working for the organization?

_____

_____

_____

This exercise was designed to open your imagination and help you bypass any fixed assumptions you may have about how your work is organized. If members of your team are working through these exercises with you, the next step is to sit down with them, or others in your organization, to see if you can come up with a team vision. Try to express your responses to these questions in one or two paragraphs and answer the following additional questions:

I. What is unique about us?

_____

_____

_____

2. What values, goals, and priorities do we have for the next several years?

_____

_____

_____

3. What would make us personally commit our minds and hearts to this team or organization?

_____

_____

_____

4. What does the organization really need that our team can and should provide?

_____

_____

_____

5. What do I want our team to accomplish so I will feel committed, aligned, and proud of my association with it?

_____

_____

_____

What will actually change in the future is unimaginable today, but it is clear that we will all be required to possess new sets of skills, adjust to new ways of thinking, learn new technologies, and engage in new behaviors that most of us never learned or experienced before. One of our clients, a mid-level manager at AT&T, coined what we call "the trash can" approach to help clear the decks for a truly new vision. She put it this way:

We need to throw out everything we know. We have to let go of what we know and start with a blank slate. It is so easy to continue what we are used to doing and just use our existing mind-set. What happens when people hear about reengineering or change is they usually take what they have and just rearrange it. We need to take a trash can and throw it all out so we can think in open, non-political, nonthreatening ways.

"Change Is Mandatory—Only Growth Is Optional"

Adam Urbanski, president of the Rochester Federation of Teachers, made this statement to illustrate the point that change *will* happen, but growth will take place only if there is willingness, choice, and involvement. Many of the reengineering companies we work with tell us they have successfully restructured lines of reporting, redesigned work processes, and installed new computer systems, yet feel they are stuck because the human beings in the organization, the people who need to buy into the change, have not been able to alter their behaviors or attitudes. Here are 10 behavioral challenges their employees say they face in trying not only to change, but also to grow:

1. **Supporting risk-taking.** "How do you convince others that they can take risks, that they will not be reprimanded by their boss and the hierarchy?"

2. **Creating consensus.** "How do you convince people to move in a common direction, with a common set of goals? How can they build teamwork? Right now they all seem to be in a different organization with everyone doing their own thing."

3. **Building skills.** "I am concerned about people issues. How do we identify functions that we need and then match them fairly with the people we have and their skills?"

4. **Improving communication.** "Communication is a big one for us. When and how is it best to communicate? For example, a memo went out from the team leader that ticked everyone off by the wording. He didn't check it out with the rest of us so there was a backlash from the customers."

5. **Increasing participation.** "Everyone needs to understand the project and what it is about. When we talk about reengineering and change, people first think downsizing and they don't want to cooperate. There is a barrier to participation, and it is fear."

6. **Improving cross-functional cooperation.** "Managing cross-functional teams was a problem for me because we did not keep the lines of communication open. The roles were not clearly defined, and the right people were not necessarily at the table."

7. **Reducing turfism.** "Politics is a continual problem. Turfism must go."

8. **Sparking innovation.** "There are barriers to people stepping away from how we do things today. I need to know how to get them to change their philosophy. I want them to question everything they are doing, to keep asking why, why, why."

9. **Supporting empowerment.** "There is a problem convincing people with authority to make changes based on team recommendations. Usually if it fits in the agenda of the

higherups, they will go with it, but most of the time we have to prove ours is the right way to go."

10. **Continuing to challenge performance.** "I get bored from time to time and need to refresh my soul."

How often do you feel your soul needs refreshing? Our souls are refreshed not by change, but by growth. It is not enough just to change the surface of things; the change must result in deep personal and organizational transformation if the problems we are experiencing are going to be solved. The problems identified by these employees are common to many organizations, yet each one is solvable.

Focusing on Growth

In our many years of work with changing organizations we have found a few very simple strategies that greatly increase the chances for growth and success of any organizational change effort. These are:

1. Include all employees in defining the organization's vision, goals, and process.
2. Empower them to solve their problems.
3. Allow them to become self-directed.
4. Train them in team process, consensus, and conflict resolution.
5. Encourage cooperation, feedback, and teamwork throughout the process.

These goals are not utopian or idealistic, but pragmatic strategies that are required to transform existing behaviors. They are not limited to corporations or to a single type of workplace. They are not "touchy feely" exercises, but practical and efficient elements in any successful change effort. The power of these strategies was expressed by one of our clients who is the leader of a highly creative, self-directed team for an entertainment industry firm:

The beauty of it is that now we have great managers, our staff is having a ball, there is high morale, we are excited about the project, we feel the company is behind it. Now that we've solved our staffing problems, we'll go off and do it. I've never had a better time in my life!

Empowered work environments that follow these strategies produce genuine, practical results, not out of fear or obedience, but through the increased motivation and teamwork that flows from them. These environments reduce the rigidity and moderate the stultifying effects of excessive centralization and hierarchy; they bring principles of democratic participation and self-governance into the workplace and thereby into the economy; and they make the workplace more pleasurable and self-fulfilling for everyone, managers as well as employees. They regularly achieve these results in many different work environments, in Fortune 500 companies, small, family-owned businesses, labor unions, public schools, community and political organizations, social service agencies, hospitals, and government departments.

One of our clients, Dave, a young team leader with a cable television finance organization, describes his work experience as an example of what is possible in this new environment:

> *Our team loves coming to work. We rave about our jobs. No one on the team says that they work for me, they work with me. We are never dictatorial, we run a pretty good democracy. They have fun, even at its craziest, you can have fun. It's a very motivated group; I have the dream team. We even spend time together outside of work playing in the same volleyball league. We love being together. I can see that in the dynamics of a team no one person will ever let the team down. It's like in the war movies, people go off and fight for their buddies; that's why they risk their lives. We have that kind of team here.*

Until Dave's organization transformed itself, his team had a fairly routine job of collecting, recording, and tracking payments of cable affiliates. Now the team creates deals, designs value-added services for their sales counterparts, and manages a new computer system that provides powerful information and impacts the bottom line of the entire company. And everyone is having fun!

Russ Ackoff, professor emeritus of the Wharton School, describes this new world in his book, *The Democratic Corporation, A Radical Prescription for Recreating Corporate America and Rediscovering Success*, as a "democratic" or "circular" type of organization:

> *In this type of organization all members can participate directly or indirectly in decisions that affect them, and there is no ultimate authority. . . . Such an organization enables people to do as well as they know how, to develop, and to have fun.*

Many organizations have learned to change the way they work and to have more fun, partly by eliminating externally imposed disciplinary rules and substituting internally motivated self-directed goals; partly by encouraging the development of leadership skills at all levels of the organization and in all aspects of its work; and partly by learning techniques for resolving workplace conflicts in ways that encourage listening and growth rather than defensiveness and dissension.

Making these changes means shifting the organizational context or paradigm from command and control to motivation and self-direction. What a context and a paradigm are and how they can be changed or shifted is the focus of the next two chapters.

TWO

Changing the Context of Work

The business community keeps on 'downsizing,' 'rightsizing,' 're-engineering' and otherwise firing people. Business consultant Michael Hammer told Newsweek, 'An enormous amount of the downsizing and restructuring in the last 10 years was foolish and a waste of energy.' We know. Anyone who has worked for a corporation long enough to watch it go through management fads—zero-based budgeting, the Z theory, Total Quality Management, etc.—knows that corporate managers are amazingly subject to the monkey-see, monkey-do syndrome. Their triumphant tendency to rediscover the wheel never ceases to amaze. I know guys who made the astounding discovery that the most successful companies in America treat their employees really well. Imagine.

MOLLY IVINS

Change Is Constant

You may be in the midst of a change effort that feels like one of the management fads Molly Ivins laments. Despite the significant improvements many of these management fads have made in the workplace, the underlying truth is that at the bottom of every successful change effort there is some humanization of the work process, some tangible improvement in the way we are treated. If we are responded to with respect, we tend to pass it on to others, and if we are not, we pass that on too.

Many of the management fads employees complain about are a result of encouraging managers to achieve short-term results, even at the risk of losing long-term advantages. New managers often seek to distinguish themselves from their predecessors by dismantling prior management programs that were achieving good results in order to substitute their own, in a new, improved, *"program du jour."*

While we are all attracted to fads and quick fixes, we also enjoy routine, even to the point of turning it into a rut. Yet change is constant, even in our personal lives. No matter how much we may wish to freeze life, to hold on to an idea or a relationship, or to keep a good job forever, change constantly drives us forward. As Omar Khayam pointed out in The Rubiyat, *"The moving finger, having writ, moves on, nor all thy piety nor wit shall lure it back to cancel half a line."*

The choice we face is not whether to change, but how to handle the change when it occurs. We all grow older, but if we fight the aging process, we make ourselves unhappy, not younger. All organizations need to adapt to changing conditions, but if they lose sight of the need to treat people humanely and respectfully, they will forget that it is not just organizations and programs that need to change, but the people who make them happen.

"They Forgot the Human Side of Change"

This complaint is the one we hear most frequently when we enter changing organizations. We often find that the managers who are actively pursuing a line of change have not taken the time, devoted the energy, or lack the skills to include their employees in the change process.

Given the pressures of global competition, the power of new technologies, the demands of customers and their changing needs, the seduction of downsizing and new mergers and acquisitions, change is always a reality in today's organizations, and will be an increasing pressure for the foreseeable future as economic globalization continues.

We often ask employees and managers, "Where is your organization? Please point to it." They suddenly realize that they *are* the organization. The key to all successful organizational change is, simply, to consider the human beings and treat them well, as they are the ones who will guide the change and make it successful.

The Constancy of Change: An Exercise

Take a moment now to think about the changes you have already experienced during your career. One or more of the approaches listed below may look familiar to you. You might want to check off the changes you have experienced in the last 10 years. If you have checked more than five, your experience is fairly normal, and probably, like everyone else, you are exhausted by change! If you have not checked any, your organization may be out of step with the times and overdue for a major systems overhaul.

1. Changes in Your Workplace

___ ◆ **Reengineering.** All your work processes have been redesigned.

___ ◆ **Mergers and acquisitions.** You've been on the buy side or the sell side of business combinations, and you've experienced the resulting culture clashes, downsizing, and restructuring.

___ ◆ **Total quality management.** Your organization has made a commitment to continuous improvement in the quality of its products and processes.

___ ◆ **Employee stock ownership plans.** You've been given an economic and personal ownership stake in your company.

___ ◆ **Self-managing teams.** You've been empowered to make decisions and work with your colleagues in a team environment, and your compensation is partly based on your team's success.

___ ◆ **Celebration of diversity.** You are encouraged and supported in valuing co-workers who are different from you racially, culturally, in gender or sexual orientation, as well as in ideas, skills, styles, and personalities.

___ ◆ **Collaborative partnerships.** You are working in partnerships with colleagues from different parts of the organization who have contrasting skills, experience, and goals.

___ ◆ **Conflict resolution systems design.** You are engaged in investigating the types of conflicts you have and their origins, and in preventing and resolving workplace disputes through mediation and other processes.

2. Changes in Your Schools

___ ◆ **School-based management.** Your school has a local site council that makes the decisions that impact the day-to-day life of your school.

___ ◆ **Shared decision making.** Parents, teachers, administrators, and classified staff collaborate in your school's management.

___ ◆ **Meaningful parent involvement.** Parents participate actively in classroom learning activities and in-home support for school work.

___ ◆ **Child-centered learning.** You are shifting your focus from what the teacher says to what the child discovers through active, curiosity based personal experiences.

___ ◆ **Constructivist curriculum.** You use learning materials that enable learners to build from what they already know or the questions they ask to discover new ideas and skills.

___ ◆ **Team teaching.** You are part of an interdisciplinary team of teachers planning together and sharing students, materials, and an integrated subject matter.

___ ◆ **Peer mediation and peer counseling.** You are working with students so that peers resolve their own disputes and counsel each other in working on their emotional problems.

___ ◆ **Authentic assessment.** You evaluate what children do and know through ongoing, hands-on, experiential activities.

3. Changes in Your Public Social Service Agencies

___ ◆ **Customer service focus.** Your agency now treats clients as partners, rather than as passive recipients.

___ ◆ **Multiple service integration.** You provide "one stop shopping" by integrating services at a single location to meet family needs.

___ ◆ **Community advisory boards.** You create entities through which you solicit community feedback and input into policy and encourage greater community participation.

___ ◆ **Accountability measures.** You are held accountable for delivery of services and have greater responsibility and authority for decision making.

___ ◆ **Accessible delivery of services.** You have decentralized services and deliver them to sites where the clients are located in schools, community centers, and accessible store-front locations.

___ ◆ **Regulation negotiation and public policy mediation.** You use negotiation, mediation, and consensus-building activities to create new public regulations and resolve community disputes, and you encourage community members to collaborate across wide-ranging differences of opinion.

___ ◆ **Automated information retrieval and delivery.** You use technology to gain the advantage of rapid access to client records and make possible a holistic approach to providing services.

___ ◆ **Interdisciplinary teams for emergencies.** You work as part of short-term, interdisciplinary "swat" teams to respond to emergencies and disasters.

If you have not experienced some of these changes, you may want to consider whether they might be useful in your workplace, either alone or as a part of a larger, overall change strategy, such as the one we are recommending here. The success of each of these change efforts depends, in large measure, on whether they incorporate the needs and experiences of all the people who need to be involved in order to make it work, and whether the organization is genuinely committed to making the change deep, substantive, and long lasting.

The Mismanagement of Change

When we ignore the human dimension, the power of the change process evaporates and disappears and the change is mismanaged. For example, to soften the effects of a proposed change or disguise its true implications, an organization may present the change in such a way as to understate its real significance, thereby not engaging the support of those who have the passion to make it succeed. Or there may be a lack of genuine commitment or leadership behind the change so that people become confused and demoralized. Or considerable attention may be paid to planning while implementation is allowed to fall through the cracks. Or attention may be given to cosmetic or superficial alterations while major problems are ignored so that new words are bandied about while old behaviors continue. Or there may be a lack of will power to see the change through to the very end so that it dies, not with a bang but a whimper. Or some new change is introduced, fast on the heels of another change, without giving adequate time for the first change to work. Or the training or support that is vitally needed for the change to work is withheld, or given too late in the process to support those who are trying to make it succeed.

Often, these results occur for reasons that have nothing to do with the usefulness of the proposed change. Sometimes change is intentionally mismanaged in order to divert attention from a failure of leadership or insufficient planning, to exert personal power over others, to get rid of internal opponents, or simply to give shareholders the impression that something important is happening. Most often, change is mismanaged because of a lack of preparation and inadequate commitment to the people who are the only ones who can make it succeed. Whatever the reason, the result is a failure of leadership and committed vision.

The leaders of organizations often mismanage the change process by promulgating a kind of superficial or *"faux* change" to substitute for their lack of true vision or courage; to give a semblance of doing something while maintaining the status quo; to convince employees to work harder without additional compensation; or to disguise a lack of genuine commitment to make deep, substantive, lasting, or constructive changes. A September 24, 1995, article in the *New York Times* reporting on the current rash of acquisitions and mergers in the entertainment industry quoted Warren Bennis:

> *I can't recall a time when there has been so much turbulence and uncertainty about what will happen. No one can clearly articulate a vision, and in lieu of vision they are buying things and selling things.*

The article by Judith Dombrzynski went on to observe:

> *Many of those chief executives also have faced complaints about performance, management style or stock price—at a time when expectations for C.E.O.'s are*

higher than ever, "When you get to be C.E.O. people expect you to make grand moves," [James O'Toole, vice president of the Aspen Institute] commented. "They're paying you a lot of money, and this is a way to strut your stuff. A lot of deals are a substitute for hard, day-to-day management of a company. The funny thing is, a deal does deflect criticism. Often, the company's stock price goes up." Seduced by the boldness of a move, and wanting to believe in its purported brilliance, Wall Street rewards the chief executive or at least cuts him some slack. "It buys you time, makes you look forceful, makes you look like a visionary," Mr. O'Toole said.

Why do these results occur so frequently during the change process? In part, because the people who make the change happen on the ground level, on a day-to-day basis are not taken into consideration at the time the decision to change is made. Their ideas, experiences, assumptions, expectations, needs, desires, and fears are not factored into the decision. If a change is going to work and something new is to be born, something old must die, including the habits of the old organization, the ways everything used to get done.

We are often reluctant to surrender these old ideas, beliefs, and habits, even when they no longer take us where we want to go. Any organization that is undergoing a merger or acquisition or outsourcing or downsizing needs to accept the human consequences of the changes they are making, and not just disguise the enormity of the change through small modifications of language or procedure.

An internal consultant at General Motors recently told us that to ameliorate to the debilitating effects of downsizing, an executive had decided to address the problem by changing the term managers were using to discuss cuts in staff from "downsizing" to "rightsizing," which, of course, did not solve the problem and, in fact, made many people feel worse about what they were doing because a lie was hidden in the new phrase. They were getting rid of staff, yet they were not honestly acknowledging the pain of the process or giving people a chance to talk about their unhappiness or respond creatively to their fears. The change allowed managers to paper over these difficulties with a word that neutralized the effect of what they were doing.

Managing the Human Side of Change

To avoid the disappointment of superficial change and increase the effectiveness of efforts to bring about a substantive transformation in the way we work, we need to examine more closely the ways we think and feel about our work, and why. No matter what anyone prescribes, including us, change cannot take hold or make a difference if we ignore the way we mentally organize our work.

We arrange our thoughts and feelings about work into mental patterns that give them meaning as a way of explaining them to ourselves. For example, we may develop a mental pattern in which we need to compete fiercely with all our colleagues and try to diminish their ideas and successes. Or we may develop a pattern of always accepting whatever our bosses tell us and not questioning authority, even if the ideas are irrelevant or doomed to failure. These patterns, which we will call *contexts*, are useful in understanding the meaning of our work experiences and making them comprehensible. It is only when these contexts change for everyone involved that major transformations become possible.

Someone defined a miracle as "a change of perception." We have seen miracles happen when people's perceptions and contexts begin to shift. We worked, for example, with an information systems group at a large west coast company. The staff was operating in an old customer service context that said, in the language of one employee:

Customers get in the way. Keep them at a distance with technical language, throw solutions over the transom and let them holler, and promise to deliver the new application a year later than realistic so that you have time to debug it.

Owing to a large volume of customer complaints and increasing competition, the members of the staff had to change their definition of who their customers were and how they would be treated. The new context they fashioned to meet the challenge of customer service stated:

The customer is our partner. Time needs to be set aside so we can respond rapidly to customer demands. We need to over-communicate and build bridges to the customer.

The resulting change in their behavior was so powerful and pervasive that several institutional customers who had temporarily been assigned to the group as resource people elected to remain as permanent team members, even though it meant becoming part of a business unit that gave them lower status than they had in their home departments!

This transformation took place only because the definition of the new context for the customer was so distinct from the old one and so powerful that it completely reshaped these employees' work experiences and performance. To create similar experiences for ourselves, we need to discover the mental contexts we use to define our work, learn how to create alternate contexts, and find out how we can alter these contexts, overcome our natural resistance to change and to help us move in the direction we desire.

The Definition of Contexts and Paradigms

What is a context? We believe that a *context* is simply a set of assumptions about our relationship with our environment. A *paradigm* is a mental framework, a pattern in the way we think about and see the world, a way of explaining its meaning. We find it useful to separate paradigms, which refer to what we think about something, from contexts, which refer to our relationship to it. For example, the idea that the earth is flat was a paradigm that created a context of fear for navigators in which sailing far away from land was seen as suicidal. Or, the loss of sailors' lives at sea was the context that led to an explanation or paradigm that gave meaning to the experience. Our ideas of the world affect our relationship to it, and our relationship to the world affects our ideas about it. Some other words that are sometimes used to describe a context or paradigm are:

Theory	Value
Model	Routine
Belief system	Habit
Protocol	Custom
Convention	Superstition
Methodology	Ritual
Prejudice	World view
Philosophy	Conformity
Givens	Truth

It is as difficult for us to perceive our contexts and paradigms as it is for a fish to perceive the water in which it swims. To us, a context may be so old and familiar that we can't imagine looking at our problems from any different perspective. It is always easier to identify a context or paradigm that is widely recognized to be outmoded than it is to see one in which we are currently operating. How do contexts and paradigms become so engrained? Why do we need to be concerned with contexts and paradigms? What is the source of their power?

* Contexts and paradigms are hidden assumptions or givens that influence the way we see our work, our relationships, and ourselves.

- They give shape to our thoughts and behavior and meaning and coherence to our experience.
- They enable us to order the data that we absorb through our senses. They provide a framework for our random thoughts.
- They glue our words together into meaningful concepts and phrases. For example, when we hear the word *work*, we may each assign different meanings to that word based on the context of our past experiences or expectations.
- They also limit our experiences by restricting our awareness of what is happening in the present and of what is possible in the future.
- They establish and limit the range of permissible perceptions, understandings, self-definitions, relationships, interactions; techniques and skills; successes and failures; and identification of problems that we can entertain.
- They even limit our recognition that a context or paradigm may be changing, and our ability to correct what failure, in another context, is obviously not working.

During periods of history in which organizational contexts or political, social, and scientific paradigms were widely accepted, few people were aware that these motions were only temporary mental constructs, rather than "The Truth." It is only through the changes that have taken place over long periods that we have been able to see that shifts have occurred away from what we once thought was unquestionable. For example, here are some major historical contexts or paradigms that have changed over the course of many years:

Old Context or Paradigm	New Context or Paradigm
1. Kings rule by divine right.	Political leadership is based on merit, on skill, and on ideas.
2. The earth is flat.	The earth is oval.
3. Slavery is justifiable based on the inferiority of the slave.	Slavery is unjustifiable because all human beings are equal.
4. Space and time are absolute.	Space and time are relative.
5. Women are incapable of voting responsibly.	Everyone is entitled to vote. One person, one vote.
6. War is the only way to settle international conflicts.	Mediation is a humane and lasting way of settling conflicts.
7. Democracy means mob rule.	Democracy means political stability.

8. It is impossible for us to get to the moon.	We have traveled to the moon and may someday colonize it.	
9. Spare the rod and spoil the child.	Children respond better to respect and love than they do to physical pain.	
10. The cold war will never end.	The cold war is over.	

Notice that each of the "truths" on the left was deeply believed in, thought to be valid for all time, and accepted for many years by many people, yet all these contexts have changed fundamentally. Looking over this list, we need to ask ourselves which of today's contexts and paradigms we may someday see as utterly illogical and unbelievable.

Contexts We Create in Our Lives: An Exercise

We will start by focusing on contexts, and then examine paradigms in greater detail in the next chapter. The following exercise is a way for you to become more aware of some of the contexts you use to guide your own thoughts, feelings and actions. You may not be aware of some of your concepts. Use your reflection to expand your awareness. In the left column below, list your contexts for each of the suggested categories. On the right side of the page, list some of the alternative contexts that *might* be true, even if you don't currently believe in them or operate within them. We have given some examples for each area. You need not subscribe to any of the alternatives we have listed or agree with them. You need only brainstorm the possibilities.

	Current Contexts	Examples	Alternative Contexts
Work	is drudgery	is fun	_____
Family	is a burden	is a source of energy	_____
Health	will disintegrate over time	gets better and better	_____
Self	my own worst enemy	my best friend	_____
Play	is only for vacations	is a part of everyday life	_____
Co-workers	are my competition	are my teammates	_____
Boss	is a micromanager	is a leader	_____

Once you notice that there are other ways of seeing the same functions and roles, you may see contexts more as personal choices, rather than as absolutes about how you are going to experience the world. These choices are also self-fulfilling prophecies, since thinking of your co-workers as competitors will encourage them to respond to you in a competitive way. Through self-examination, dialogue, and experimentation, you can start to see your own contexts more distinctly. Once you see them clearly, you are freer to chose alternative ways of experiencing the world.

We all know people who express their views forcefully. We know the president of a small service organization who is so convinced of the truth of her "position" that all the information she receives gets twisted to fit and support her context. It is impossible to suggest any other way of seeing the world to her. She has been very effective at using her self-confidence and single-mindedness to overcome lethargy and apathy inside her organization. But she is also a prisoner of her own context, and is unable to appreciate fresh ideas or understand how others might view the same phenomenon differently; she is locked into a narrow range of possibilities. The ability to see outside our own ideas allows us to choose between alternative contexts, which enables us to be more flexible and empathetic and to adjust our assumptions to a rapidly changing reality.

We do not consciously create the contexts we adopt. They arise naturally out of patterns of thinking and social pressures to conform that begin in our earliest years. It is useful and important in looking at our work contexts to think about whether we have adopted someone else's ideas or contexts without really examining them carefully. It is difficult for us to distinguish the contexts we have consciously accepted or created and those we have not, as most of us adopt a context by passive acceptance, especially in the workplace.

Discovering Our Contexts

So how do we change a context we are not fully aware of that nonetheless controls our experiences? We need to begin by noticing the gaps, cracks, anomalies, conflicts, and discrepancies that are present in our current lives, and be courageous enough to explore them. The novelist Annie Dillard writes movingly of what can be found in these gaps:

The gaps are the thing. The gaps are the spirit's own home, the altitudes and latitudes so dazzlingly spare and clean that the spirit can discover itself like a once-blind man unbound. The gaps are the clefts in the rock where you cower to see the back parts of God; they are the fissures between mountains and cells the wind lances through, the icy narrowing fjords splitting the cliffs of mystery. Go up into the gaps. If you can find them; they shift and vanish too. Stalk the gaps. Squeak into a gap in the soil, turn and unlock—more than a maple—a universe.

A nonrational, "gut" reaction often gives us the first information that our old context is no longer working. The logical thought patterns of the left hemisphere of the brain tend to reinforce our existing contexts, while the more intuitive and artistic right hemisphere tends to challenge them. We need to pay close attention to the information we receive from our intuitive, nonlinear minds and look for clues that a context has begun to change.

The appearance of conflict is often a signal that a context needs to be reexamined. Sometimes the conflict presents itself as a clear disagreement between the "facts" and the "explanation," and sometimes it is simply a sense of unease about minor points that don't quite fit the picture we have about "the way it should be."

For example, in a work setting in which self-directed teams have recently been established, conflicts frequently arise between managers and employee teams regarding control over the work process. The context has formally shifted to place responsibility for work in the hands of employee teams, yet the manager has not made a corresponding shift in his or her style of management. The conflict is actually a sign that is pointing directly at the need to create a new way of managing and assessing performance. By bringing the parties together to resolve this conflict, the need for a new context for management will become apparent to everyone. If we do not want to be stuck in conflicts reflecting a contrast between old and new contexts, we need to become more sensitive to information that does not fit, and learn to see conflict as the voice of the new context.

For example, we worked for more than a year with a leadership group in the television industry. Most of the managers were strong leaders in their particular areas, able to produce good results with their own employees, but unwilling to work together or operate as a team. The old context was that the individual was all-powerful and driven to succeed, even if it meant killing off everyone on the team. It wasn't until a conflict arose when one member of the leadership group became so negative and disruptive that the group finally had to look at its assumptions. By taking him on, confronting his dysfunctional behavior, and seeing that one person could demolish the group's objectives, the team members saw that they had *all* been operating as mini-monarchs. The context cracked, and deep changes began to happen.

One of the central sources of conflict we see in our clients' organizations are the anomalies that arise between the old tradition of hierarchical, authoritarian, command-and-control management, and the new self-directed, team-based, collaborative, and democratic model. Our belief is that this new context, which motivates each person to improve him or herself, is generating a fundamental change in the way we think about and manage the work process that has consequences for every aspect of our work.

Alternative Contexts and Paradigms for Work

Identifying the contexts we have created, or those we have passively accepted, is not at all an easy matter particularly in the workplace where we enter a culture in which others have largely set the rules, policies, procedures, and contexts. On the next page we have given a few examples of traditional workplace contexts and paradigms, contrasted with alternatives drawn from some of the structural changes that are now taking place in the workplace.

At a recent gathering of community leaders from Africa, Latin America, and the United States concerned with alleviating poverty, our friend from Mexico, Gustavo Estava, an internationally known critic of development policies and a community leader, posed an interesting alternative to our context of poverty. He said we tend to see poverty as a lack of something, which leads us to provide those who are poor with money, services, or resources. If we can instead see poverty as a result of some circumstance, action, or situation, alleviating poverty would mean supporting poor communities in removing the circumstances that created the poverty. Rather than providing welfare, the focus would shift to removing discrimination in hiring; increasing jobs and educational opportunities; and empowering communities to find the money, services, and resources they lack. With a small change in the context, we can generate a world of new strategies and behaviors.

Traditional Context or Paradigm	Alternative Context or Paradigm
Individual performance.	Team performance.
Work is repetitive.	Work is varied.
Organizations are hierarchical.	Organizations are democratic.
Staff composition is uniform.	Staff composition is diverse.
Command and control management.	Consensus based leadership.
Staff are managed.	Staff are leaders.
Focus on product.	Focus on customer.
Tools are mainframes.	Tools are laptops.
Send a memo.	Send an e-mail.
Marketplace is national.	Marketplace is global.
Job security.	Job flexibility.
In-house shop.	Outsourcing.
Single task.	Multiple tasks.
Top-down evaluation.	360-degree evaluation.
Commute to work.	Telecommute.

Workplace Contexts: An Exercise

What are some of the contexts that are operating in your workplace? What are the assumptions that underlie the decisions you make and the way you organize your work? Write down the existing contexts that operate in your work and then try to create alternative contexts that you would like to see accepted.

Do you see anything in common between the contexts in any of these areas? What do they mean for the way we think about and organize our work lives? Why do the alternatives seem more attractive to you than the ones you have been using to guide your work? Do the new contexts you created reinforce each other?

It is not easy to question the truths we have grown accustomed to, as they are assumptions on which we have built our lives. It is much easier to stay with the old contexts and defend them—sometimes to our death. Organizational contexts often interact to create a mutually reinforcing system. If you change one, any or all of them may shift, yet each one also supports the others, making it more difficult to break through the system to create a new way of organizing work.

	Current Workplace Contexts	Alternative Workplace Contexts
Who Hires		
Who Fires		
Who Makes Policy Decisions		
Who Gets Rewarded		
Who Gets Punished		
Who Gets Promoted		
Who Leads		
Who Follows		
Who Controls Communication		
Who Resolves Conflicts		
Who Receives Training		
Who Speaks		
Who Listens		
Who Has Access to Financial Information		

Opportunity Knocks

Sometimes the key to a major organizational transformation occurs when a small, seemingly insignificant context is challenged. For example, we often think of employees who complain or knock ideas for change as negative thinkers or as troublemakers or as people with attitude problems. Yet as

Michael Maccoby reported in a *Harvard Business Review* article entitled "Different Teams for Different Folks," the context that expresses the way we treat each other in the workplace differs from culture to culture:

> When I visited the Toyota assembly plant at Nagoya (Japan), I was told that there were an average of 47 ideas per worker per year of which 80 percent were adopted. I couldn't believe it; this meant almost an idea from each worker every week. The Toyota manager said, "I think you in the West have a different view of ideas. What you call complaints, we call ideas. You try to get people to stop complaining. We see each complaint as an opportunity for improvement."

The shift in perception that redefines a complaint as an opportunity for improvement is a small change that can leverage an enormous transformation in the way we work. It redefines our work as a mutual responsibility, as a team project, as a source of self-actualization, pride, and learning. It redefines complaining as pointing to what is not working and redefines change as listening creatively to complaints. The consequences of this shift in thinking go far beyond the workplace.

When the *Challenger* space shuttle blew up, the resulting investigation revealed that Morton Thiokol employees had installed faulty o-rings because they were not willing to speak up or take responsibility for admitting that a mistake had been made and that there was a problem with the parts they had created. Group think and the suppression of criticism are part of the old hierarchical context that views complaints as troublemaking. While teams can also become sources of conformity and "group think," genuine self-directed teams do not suppress their mistakes, but require each of their members to take full responsibility for all the problems and for resolving them. As one team member told us:

> It is hard to let my teammates down. I find myself staying later and working harder to deliver for them. In the old world, I could shuffle and fake it. Now they call me on those moves when I fall back into my old ways.

We all pay a high price when we operate blindly in an unexamined context. In *Pygmalion in the Classroom*, a classic study conducted by Harvard psychologists Robert Rosenthal, Florence Shelton, and Bernard Bruce, teachers in two classrooms were assigned students with the same I.Q.s, ages, socioeconomic, and racial backgrounds, but told that one group tested much higher than the other in intelligence. Both teachers taught the same curriculum. By the end of the year, the students whose teacher expected them to test higher did much better in grades, I.Q scores, and self-esteem than the other students, and the teacher was much happier with her experience than the teacher of the other group. The context each teacher accepted of the intelligence of her class determined how she treated them, which determined how they learned and performed, and how they treated her in return. We cycle from using data to reinforce our concepts to using our concepts to shape the data, which keeps us locked in and blind to alternative ideas and behaviors.

Changing the Context and Shifting the Paradigm

Our purpose in this book is to call attention to emerging new contexts of work. In our experience, many organizations are moving away from old patterns of homogeneity, hierarchy, and obedience and embracing new patterns based on heterogeneity, participatory democracy, and self-direction. The contrasting ideas we have listed below highlight some of the shifts that we believe are emerging in the way our clients work:

Where We Have Been	Where We May Be Going
The future is predictable.	The future is unpredictable.
Change is slow.	Change is rapid.
Power is at the top of the hierarchy.	Customers and employees have power.
Work is routine.	Work is improvisational.
Uniformity is necessary.	Diversity is essential.
Employees need discipline.	Employees can discipline themselves.
Criticism means disloyalty.	Criticism leads to improvement.
Details are controlled.	Details are left to discretion.
Centralize and merge.	Decentralize and divest.
Do it internally.	Outsource it.
Evaluation is arbitrary.	Evaluation is authentic.
Quantity over quality.	Quality and quantity.
Leaders are those with titles.	Leaders are those who are followed.
Conflict is suppressed.	Conflict is used to learn and change.

Several common themes appear in these new contexts or paradigms. There is greater power, flexibility, and responsibility on the part of employees who operate less in isolation and more as members of a team; the distinction between employee and manager becomes blurred as both become leaders; employees have a stronger voice in running the enterprise, and may have an ownership interest or share in the distribution of profits; and the work relationship shifts from one of coercion, control, suspicion, monitoring, and punishment to one of consensus, creativity, trust, peer feedback, and reward.

The steps we need to take to change from the old contexts to the new ones are not orderly or linear. Organizations often move back and forth between becoming more aware of their problems, having insights into possible solutions, taking action, reflecting on their results, and gaining new insights all over again. In our experience, changes in context usually go through the following steps, though not necessarily in this order:

1. Becoming aware of anomalies, inconsistencies, and conflicts that define the weakness of the old context.
2. Becoming aware of the patterns in these anomalies, seeing them as pointing to the old context, being able to name it and describe it.
3. Noticing a new configuration of information or learning that includes a new and more effective way of perceiving and explaining our experiences.
4. Articulating this new perspective to ourselves and then to others.
5. Testing the new ideas in action to see if the new ways of thinking are valid across a broad range of experience.
6. Restating the new context based on the results of that experience and on feedback and interaction with others.
7. Convincing others of the validity of the new context and gradually consolidating their acceptance.
8. Beginning to notice anomalies, inconsistencies, and conflicts in the new contexts and beginning the process all over again!

Shifting the Context: An Exercise

The following exercise may help you notice some of your organization's anomalies, identify its old contexts, notice the new configurations, and articulate a new context. By yourself, or with a group at work, please complete the following chart, using your own workplace as an example.

Shifting Contexts	Old Context	New Context
1. Beliefs about the Nature of Work		
2. Views of the Role of the Individual		
3. Definitions of Success and Failure		

The most interesting way for you to explore old and new contexts through this activity is to work with others and compare your perceptions. If several small groups are working on this exercise, each group should complete the chart on its own and then share their findings. If there is a great deal of common ground in each group's descriptions, you have a consensus of perception and are probably ready to shift your organizational context, or it may have already shifted. If there is no agreement among these groups or individuals, you may need more discussion, more exploration, and perhaps some facilitation or conflict resolution to come to a common understanding.

Charting a Cultural Change

We recently used the preceding exercise with a group of 25 directors of a large organization in the throes of fundamental structural and cultural change. The charts on the next page represent their work on organizational change. You can create different headings for your context charts based on the issues your organization needs to address in order to change. These · directors represented 10 departments, and their shared goal was to improve motivation, efficiency, and leadership. We divided them into three teams to analyze their old and new cultures. In the charts presented on the following page, you can see the different ideas expressed by each team.

Notice that while the wording of some of these observations varies from chart to chart, the concepts are quite similar. There is a sense of congruence or common direction among the 25 directors. This level of agreement gave us permission to begin planning a transition from the old to the new context, and to explore the implications of these context shifts in terms of how work is done, how staff is organized, and how behavior is rewarded. You can use this exercise in your own workplace as a way of identifying areas of hidden agreement and of connecting what people are thinking individually but have not been able to communicate to each other or act upon in concert. Because there is no such thing as a neutral observation, simply identifying a context already begins to shift it.

Sources of Resistance to the New Context

Letting go of an old context or paradigm that we know and love and shifting to a new one we do not fully understand is difficult. Resistance

	Motivation	Efficiency	Leadership

Team One

Motivation	Efficiency	Leadership
Old Motivation	**Old Efficiency**	**Old Leadership**
◆ Refuses responsibilities	◆ Work divided up to its maximum extent	◆ Autocratic
◆ Theory X		◆ Autocratic-paternalist
◆ The stick and the carrot	◆ Very well-defined functions and responsibilities	◆ Personality leadership
◆ Homo economicus		
◆ Homo lazy	◆ Mass production	
	◆ Economies of scale	
New Motivation	**New Efficiency**	**New Leadership**
◆ Search for self-realization	◆ Responsibility from beginning to end	◆ Democracy
◆ Feeling useful and recognized	◆ Social contribution	◆ Learning
◆ Participation in decision making	◆ Full productivity, including quality	◆ Transformational leadership
◆ Teamwork	◆ Sustained competitiveness	◆ Participatory
◆ Theory Y	◆ Integrated systems	◆ Team leadership
		◆ Entrepreneurship

Team Two

Motivation	Efficiency	Leadership
Old Motivation	**Old Efficiency**	**Old Leadership**
◆ Managers decide	◆ Producing an amount	◆ Centralization
◆ Money	◆ No value to the working staff	◆ Nonprofessional (without training)
◆ Individualism	◆ Wasting	◆ Centralized administrative plans
	◆ Ridged patterns	
New Motivation	**New Efficiency**	**New Leadership**
◆ According to needs	◆ Producing quality	◆ Decentralization
◆ Improved living conditions	◆ Value to the working staff	◆ More participatory
◆ A tendency to evaluate results of the whole group	◆ Saving	◆ A recognition for training
	◆ International perspective	◆ Goal management

Team Three

Motivation	Efficiency	Leadership
Old Motivation	**Old Efficiency**	**Old Leadership**
◆ Salary	◆ Rigid planned achievement	◆ Centralization
◆ Moralism		◆ Commands
◆ Loyalty	◆ Politics in production	◆ Autocracy
◆ Ideologization	◆ To achieve at any risk	◆ Formal participation
New Motivation	**New Efficiency**	**New Leadership**
◆ Goals' interrelations	◆ Optimizing resources	◆ Decentralization
◆ Real efficiency	◆ Innovations	◆ Real participation
◆ Problem solving	◆ Costs rationalizing	◆ Consensus
◆ Survival		

takes many forms in our own minds and in the reactions of others, and becomes more powerful as the potential impact on our cherished habits and assumptions becomes greater. Much of our history is the story of courageous individuals who advanced a new perception, paradigm, or context and faced powerful, often armed, rejection. Socrates, Galileo, Copernicus, Darwin, Marx, Freud, Einstein, Gandhi, Mandela, Susan B. Anthony, Cesar Chavez, Malcolm X and Martin Luther King Jr.: The list goes on and on. All found new ways of seeing the world, all were persecuted for the unpopularity of their beliefs, and many are hated to this day, irrespective of their common achievement, which was to enrich humankind with a new idea. We have immortalized the visions of many of these extraordinary thinkers, yet in their own times their ideas were rejected and they were reviled, persecuted, and sometimes assassinated.

Some of the common reasons for rejecting a new context and resisting change are listed below. As you review these phrases, think how your own managers, co-workers and colleagues respond to change, and of your organizations most popular responses to change. Also, listen to your own voice, your own inner conversations, and notice the sources of your own resistance to acting on what you know, at some deep level, is true.

Strategies for Overcoming Resistance to Changing the Context: An Exercise

Notice the phrases we have put in quotes in the following chart. They almost automatically imply a strategy for responding to each of these sources of resistance. For example, if employees are fearful that they "can't do it" or they will be inadequate, one strategy would be to create a training program to assist them to feel more comfortable and powerful in the new context. In the space provided below each type of resistance, write a strategy you think might help either yourself or others where you work get past their concerns and become more willing to accept a new context. If you are working in a group, each person may want to pick the source of resistance that is closest to his or her own heart. We always know best what will reduce our own resistance. Use this exercise to share your favorite forms of resistance with others and to open a conversation about strategies for overcoming them.

1. Fear—"I'm afraid I can't do it."

   Strategy:_____

   _____

   _____

2. Loss—"I'll miss the good old days."

   Strategy:_____

   _____

   _____

3. Anger—"I'm furious that they did that to me."

   Strategy:_____

   _____

   _____

4. Doubt—"What if it doesn't work?"

   Strategy:_____

   _____

   _____

5. Jealousy—"Somebody else is getting more than I am."

   Strategy:_____

   _____

   _____

6. Prejudice—"It won't work because they came up with it."

   Strategy:_____

   _____

   _____

7. Laziness—"It's too much trouble."

   Strategy:_____

   _____

   _____

8. Pessimism—"It didn't work before. It never works."

   Strategy:_____

   _____

   _____

9. Complacency—"I'm comfortable with the problems I know."

   Strategy:_____

   _____

   _____

10. Apathy—"It won't make any difference."

    Strategy:_____

    _____

    _____

11. Cynicism—"They are just in it for themselves."

    Strategy:_____

    _____

    _____

12. Imperfection—"There are flaws in the plan."

    Strategy:_____

    _____

    _____

Dealing with our own resistance is often the hardest part of the process. In our experience, it helps to be scrupulously honest with ourselves and with team members about our fears, denials, and dislikes.

From the exercise above, review your strategies. How many of them had to do with honest communication? Do the strategies point to a need to peel off layers of defensiveness, or do they reveal a desire to hold on to the past? What would it take to implement these strategies in your organization? We will return to this topic later in the book and give you concrete suggestions for responding to the many ways we resist change.

Summary of the Rules that Guide Context and Paradigm Shifts

Before we leave this exploration, we would like to summarize some of the rules we believe govern the process of shifting our contexts and paradigms, some of which have been drawn from the work of Thomas Kuhn, Tom Barker, and others. These rules may help you see the systems of thought that shape your own thinking and acting and help you take the time and effort needed to change the context.

1. It is not possible to force a context or paradigm to change, or to pretend one has changed when it hasn't.
2. Contexts and paradigms change because of an accumulation of conflicts, errors, anomalies, and problems that cannot be solved using the old context.
3. The people who create new contexts and paradigms are usually those who do not understand that the problem cannot be solved or that the rules cannot be changed.
4. Old contexts tend to filter out information that point to a new context and circle back on themselves to create a self-defining system.
5. Conflict is often the voice of a new context or paradigm. Conflict is an opportunity for deeper understanding and a source of energy and motivation to make the change actually happen.
6. Contexts and paradigms can be changed without people or organizations becoming dysfunctional, though it often appears that they can't.
7. Skills that enable people to be successful under the old context or paradigm do not necessarily guarantee success under the new one.

8. The more profound the context change or paradigm shift, the more it will affect both process and content, changing not only what we do but also the way we do it.

9. New contexts and paradigms automatically alter our self-concepts, along with our ideas about and relationships with others.

10. It is not possible to successfully control or manage a change in context or a shift in paradigm, or to change to a new context or paradigm, using a style or process that defined the old one. Einstein said: *"Our problems cannot be solved by the same level of thinking that created them."*

Finally, we would like to share John Welwood's discussion of paradigms in his book, *The Holographic Paradigm.* He points out that our sense of inner truth is our best guide in acknowledging the old paradigms that don't work and in finding new ones:

What moves us to accept a new paradigm, finally? Experimental data alone can never fully establish the truth of a new paradigm, for the paradigm itself orders and makes sense of the data. Are we not moved to embrace a paradigm when it somehow resonates with the richness of that we already implicitly know? In this sense, is it not perhaps our intuitive sense of the implicate order of things that encourages us to adopt it?

Listen to what you implicitly know, and your intuitive sense will tell you when and how to change your contexts and paradigms.

THREE

Understanding How We Got Here

We trained hard, but it seemed every time we were beginning to form up into teams we would be reorganized. I was to learn later in life that we tend to meet any new situation by reorganizing, and a wonderful method it can be for creating the illusion of progress while producing confusion, inefficiency and demoralization.

PETRONIUS ARBITER, ROME, 61 ACE

A Short History of Work

As you read this quotation from Roman history, you may wonder if management has ever changed! The French have expressed this feeling in a saying: *Plus ca change, plus ca c'est la meme chose.* The more things change, the more they remain the same.

When we visit our children's schools, we often find the same methods, contexts, and paradigms operating as when we were children, with teachers lecturing and children listening, with curriculum and instructional practices dictated by outside experts, and with the school run by the principal, all designed in the image of a 19th-century factory. Paradigms from our past are alive and well in our organizations!

When we interviewed several managers in a large corporate division that was embroiled in serious labor disputes and facing difficult contract negotiations, many of the people we spoke to expressed a need for both sides to reexamine the lens through which they saw their relationship, and to create a new labor/management paradigm. One of the most articulate managers said:

> *One thing that would be helpful for labor relations is more training for managers. There is a lot of concern with what is happening with our union steward. He is new and seen as aggressive. When I went to steward training conducted by the union that really helped me see him and the union differently. We have to feel more comfortable that because they are union doesn't mean the whole world has to come to a standstill. Just because the steward can be intimidating because he is a big person physically doesn't mean we have to see him and the union in the old way. I feel we need to be more successful in getting together to share problems and work on how to deal with them. This is a shift in how we see each other. We can tell our stories and realize we are not alone in how we see the world or with our failures and insecurities. This would certainly turn upside down how we view each other and our worlds.*

Most of us carry unresolved contexts and paradigms from our past that continue to shape our expectations, and limit even our sense of what it is possible for us to change. Our current problems in the workplace are not isolated events, but patterns that we can see more distinctly when we look at them from a distance that includes the way things were in the past. The contexts and paradigms of work we find ourselves stuck in now represent an accumulation of all our old, unchallenged assumptions, including all the outdated ideas and ancient conflicts on which they were based. Until we understand these old paradigms and begin to recognize their power, they will continue to limit our choices.

Our relationship with work is partly a product of the way we think about work, which is influenced largely by our personal and professional life experiences, and also by our experiences as a society over a long period of history. While it is true that the more things change the more they remain the same, it is often not the thing that needs to change, but the way we have been thinking and communicating about it. What Petronius Arbiter noticed is not just how reorganization is able to create the illusion of progress, but how an unexamined paradigm or way of thinking can create many of our problems.

We need to deepen our understanding of how work came to be organized the way it is today. To do this, we will outline six historical paradigms that have shaped our thinking and our experience of work. At the end of this chapter, we will ask you to see whether you have found any of these paradigms from the past still operating in your current organization or work environment.

Looking back over the broad course of our history, we can begin to think of work not only as functional and critical to survival, but also as a *social relationship,* and potentially as a source of satisfaction in and of itself; as a creative act that allows us to express ourselves, as a way of helping others and helping ourselves at the same time.

An enormous amount of human activity has been devoted to art, music, poetry, sports, games, scientific speculation, story-telling, debate, philosophical speculation, political dialogue, love-making, and so forth. Clearly, we do not live by bread alone, but need roses, poetry, ideas, work, and laughter as well. Yet we have largely lost this sense of work as a joyful, fulfilling end in itself, and tend to think of it more as a source of drudgery and compulsion. Part of the reason lies in the history of work and the continuation of paradigms that are no longer empowering or liberating.

As you read about the following six historical paradigms that have shaped our thinking and our experience of work, consider the paradigms you have inherited in your own life from the past, think about how they might play a role in your present, and ask yourself whether any part of your own attitude or relationship to work has been influenced, even subtlely, by these ideas. At the end of each paradigm, we will give you an example from our experience that shows how that paradigm may echo in the present. See if these stories prompt you to think of examples of your own.

Paradigm #1: Labor Is Performed by Slaves or by Disenfranchised Workers Who Can Be Treated Inhumanely

Beginning with the rise of slavery in the ancient world and continuing until today, human beings have often been seen not as the subjects, but as the *objects* of labor, as *things* to be manipulated for a profit. Slaves had no right to direct the work process or experience even the simple human pleasures of free conversation or independent action. Under feudalism, particularly after the devastation caused by the plague, serfs were legally prevented from leaving their employment for any reason without their master's consent, and were often treated inhumanely.

The Dickensian factory system that followed in the 18th and 19th centuries made slaves and serfs free in name only, and required work, even from small children, from before sunup until after sundown six days a week, with no time for recreation or renewal. Workers had no protection against abuse, and no right to even try to improve their working conditions. Those who did try were fired, beaten, spied upon, and arrested.

Like the slaves and serfs who preceded them, 18th- and 19th-century factory workers had no right to free speech or to criticize their employers; no right to strike or have a grievance heard; no right to become sick, take a vacation, or be compensated for an injury that occurred at work. To oppose this system in any way meant not only being fired, but being blacklisted as well, so that families of outspoken workers had no money to pay for food, clothing, or shelter.

In this process, a paradigm was formed. The workplace became a battleground, where the ability to work with dignity and survive was pitted against the right to control the workforce and purchase labor at the lowest possible price, resulting in an intense struggle between labor and management. From its earliest beginnings, our work lives have been controlled or managed by others, most often by individuals selected without the consent or involvement of those who performed the labor. Slavery and serfdom can be seen as early, extreme forms of autocratic management, in which the employee ceased to have any say in the work process, and became merely another form of property or wealth.

For many employees in countries around the world, and for many here at home, these problems continue to the present day. These conditions spawned widespread efforts during the late 19th and early 20th centuries to organize labor unions in an effort to secure an eight-hour day, eliminate child labor, establish public schools, and protect fundamental human rights to safety, dignity, and survival.

This paradigm is present in the workplace today whenever management fires an employee unfairly or without respecting her or his dignity; when a company fails to provide adequate safety precautions; or when an organization discriminates against employees on the basis of their race, gender, nationality, age, sexual orientation, handicap, or any reason other than whether they can do the work. It is not only the behavior that is the problem, but also an *attitude* or paradigm about employees that regards them as inferior, or undeserving of human respect.

See if you can recognize this paradigm in the following story, told to us recently by the director of an information technology department in a large insurance company. A massive layoff was planned for implementation on Monday morning without consulting or notifying anyone other than the topmost executives. As the director and her colleagues arrived at work, they were asked to come to a central staging area in the building. The names of the people being fired were read from a list. As each person's name was announced, managers took them to clean out their desks. Those who did not have cars were escorted to waiting taxi cabs to leave immediately. Many of those who were terminated had worked for the company for more than a decade. What message was communicated to those employees, and to the ones left behind, about their worth, their choices, their humanity? How might the layoff have been handled differently? What paradigm about the nature of employees was being acted upon?

Paradigm #2: Labor Needs to Be Controlled through Scientific Management and Efficiency

The militant labor battles of the late 19th and early 20th centuries led to a fundamental reorganization of work and the development of new methods of management. From Coeur d'Alene to Homestead, from Pullman to Leadville and the Great Steel Strike of 1919, the growth of labor militancy was a direct result of the oppressive environment established during the slavery era. Unions were able to use strikes and picketing effectively as techniques for winning workers' rights. Replacing skilled craft workers during a strike became difficult, since most potential strikebreakers lacked the skills to perform their work.

The increasing effectiveness of strikes forced management to restructure the workplace. Craft skills were broken down into a number of unskilled parts, each of which could be performed by unskilled laborers, who could be replaced easily during a strike. With the rise of mass production, assembly line techniques, and an increase in immigration, a seemingly unending supply of unskilled, low-paid, nonunionized labor made it possible to apply principles of scientific efficiency to problems of production.

Frederick W. Taylor was the most important spokesperson for this new efficiency theory, authoring several books, including *Principles of Scientific Management* and other studies on productivity. Taylor created and implemented this paradigm shift by applying time and motion engineering principles to the study of efficiency in work, so as to remove from skilled employees any ability to make decisions about or to control the work process. Taylor's ideas of "scientific management" are made clearer by contrasting them with more modern approaches to employee self-management:

Scientific Management	Self-Management
1. Specify the way each task is to be performed by each worker in detail.	Let those who do the work decide how best to do the job.
2. Reward each worker according to the amount produced.	Promote a collaborative approach through team rewards.
3. Encourage workers to accept detailed instructions and train rote.	Encourage workers to take responsibility and train them to think independently.
4. Management does all the thinking and workers do exactly as they are told.	Workers and managers think strategically and everyone implements.

(Source: Neal Herrick, *Joint Management and Employee Participation*)

Taylor believed that "scientific management makes collective bargaining and trade unionism unnecessary" because it substitutes external authority and discipline for self-management. Taylor established many of the basic tenets of management philosophy in his teachings, which continue to affect the way companies operate today. This paradigm of external control over the production process still operates wherever employees are excluded from full participation in the decision-making process, and where efficiency is valued over quality and service.

We have observed Taylorism's continuing impact on organizational thinking in much of our present work. One of our entertainment industry clients, for example, has experienced numerous conflicts between the artists who perform the work, creating footage for films, and the managers who try to control them, using quotas to encourage them to meet their production schedules, which made the artists furious because their creativity was being undervalued. Through an intervention, we were able to shift the paradigm of these managers from one of external direction and control to one of empowering partnerships, and get both sides to work together toward their common goals. Quotas for productivity, narrowly defined tasks, and top-down control of output are often signs of a lack of employee empowerment, and the use of a "control," rather than a "problem solving" orientation.

The idea here is not that efficiency or time-and-motion studies are improper, but that the goal of increasing output is no more important than that of treating the people whose work increases it with respect and fairness, and that these problems belong both to employees and managers. If your organization sacrifices fairness to efficiency, an outdated paradigm based on Taylor's ideas is more than likely in place.

At some point, too great a concern for efficiency ends up being inefficient. Studies have revealed that after a certain number of hours of work, an additional hour actually *reduces* productivity, and that the most productive thing an employee can do at that point is to take a break. It has also been shown that employees with high morale who are allowed to control their own work process are capable of producing a far greater output than employees whose every move is programmed and directed like those of a robot. The problem with Taylor's paradigm is that it undervalues the contributions made by employees, and therefore ends up being less efficient than self-management.

Paradigm #3: Government Has a Right to Regulate Work

A fundamental change took place in the way we think about work during the 1930s. The Depression clearly showed that private industry and market principles were incapable of solving the economic crisis, and that government had an obligation to regulate the work process in the interest of fairness to employees and consumers, as well as to provide jobs if private industry was unable to do so.

From the National Recovery Act to the Wagner Act and from the jobs creation programs of the Works Progress Administration to the Social Security Administration, government during the Depression years fundamentally altered the American workplace. The New Deal, along with the creation of industrial labor organizations such as the CIO, gave a tremendous boost to the prestige and electoral power of labor, creating a sense of rights, entitlement, and reliance on government support for working people, which coalesced politically in the Roosevelt coalition.

With the coming of World War II, government signaled the beginning of its withdrawal from active support for the rights of labor. The wartime "No Strike" agreement, passage of the Taft-Hartley Act, efforts to expel Communists from participation in labor unions, and appointment of corporate representatives and conservatives to the National Labor Relations Board were all efforts to reduce the scope of government protection afforded to labor unions. Corporate campaign contributions began to outstrip those of organized labor, prosperity returned, and the Democratic Party's "F.D.R. coalition" began slowly to unravel.

Nonetheless, the idea continued that employees were entitled to be treated with dignity and respect, and that government was obligated to protect the rights of labor. This paradigm also, however, encouraged union bureaucracy, and a tendency for employees and unions to rely on the government to step in and solve their problems, rather than being self-reliant and responsible for finding solutions themselves.

While government is excellent at enforcing minimum standards, or establishing a floor, it has a much harder time inspiring people to achieve maximum goals, or reaching for the ceiling. Government regulations have helped eliminate some of the worst behaviors under paradigms 1 and 2, and made it possible for employees in certain areas to demand that employers listen to them. But government regulations have not, and cannot, produce highly motivated, self-reliant employees. That requires employee involvement and a voluntary choice.

Many of the problems with this paradigm are evident in the workplace today. For example, much of our work is in organizational mediation, in which we are asked to help resolve disputes that might otherwise end up in litigation. One of our clients is a large government agency involved in the enforcement of labor laws that is ironically plagued with its own internal dissension. When internal disputes arise in this high-pressured, visible enforcement agency, the staff members think of going to court to resolve them, or trying to get some other governmental agency to step in and help, rather than working out their problems directly with one another.

Paradigm #4: Workers Are More Productive and Motivated When Self-Managed

This revolutionary change that has taken place in workplace paradigms really began in the last few decades, when employers started giving permission to employees to manage themselves. The turning point came when academic studies began to show that productivity is dramatically improved when employees are motivated, and a connection began to be drawn between workers' motivation and how they were treated.

These studies on motivation started with the emergence of psychology in the early part of the 20th century, and with the birth of motivational psychology as a way of understanding the actions of consumers, employees, and soldiers. Companies sought to create advertising that would attract more customers, to motivate their employees to beat the competition, and to increase their productivity. At the same time, the military sought to use psychology during World Wars I and II as a way of matching individual attitude, aptitude, and motivation with placement, training, and types of machinery.

These early studies formed part of the emerging paradigm of using motivational psychology to improve employee performance. Before World War I, Hugo Muenstenberg, a professor at Harvard University, created a test to select the best candidates to become Boston streetcar motormen. The test became a model for using industrial psychology to match individual skills with the requirements of the workplace. Meanwhile, Walter Dill Scott, a professor at Northwestern University, pioneered in the use of motivational psychology to promote products through advertising. During World War I, motivational psychologists helped train army personnel and select candidates for officer training school.

Beginning in the 1920s, the Western Electric plant in Chicago undertook a series of studies to determine the effects of specific working conditions on performance. These "Hawthorne Studies" led to an examination of "informal organization" in the workplace, and a recognition that informal work groups and informal leadership could have a substantial impact on workers' attitudes, behavior, and productivity.

Kurt Lewin took the next step in the development of this paradigm with his study of "group dynamics," which shifted emphasis away from "industrial rationalization" and time-and-motion engineers like Taylor, and focused attention on motivation and human factors. This shift paralleled the developing strength of the labor movement while diminishing reliance on technology and efficiency. Lewin believed that management models needed to be based on a workable theory of human behavior. Lewin's ideas can be summarized as follows:

Lewin's Theory	Management Implications
You can understand behavior only in relation to all the forces acting on a person at a given moment.	To change a system you must consider economics, technology, and the people who are in it.
The best way to advance knowledge is by having experts and workers study together the relations among persons, tools, and jobs.	Successful work design requires cross-functional teams of engineers, managers, and workers collaborating.
Only freely chosen work has the meaning and life value needed to motivate high performance.	People should have as much elbow room as possible in doing their own jobs.
Democratic leadership leads to higher achievement and better relationships than hands-off or authoritarian behavior.	Leading people to set goals, choose methods, and make decisions is a *learned* behavior. Nobody is born knowing participative management.
It is easier to change behavior in a group than one-on-one because norms (unwritten rules) strongly affect individual actions.	Talking over important decisions in groups *before* implementation leads to higher commitment to change.
People are more committed to solutions they have helped to design than to carrying out "expert" advice.	It is better to give people a few boundary conditions and let them solve the problem than to hand them ready-made solutions.
Every unsolved problem represents forces pushing for and against resolution. Easier and effective solutions come by reducing restraints rather than by adding pressure.	Force field analysis quickly identifies restraints to be reduced. It is effective as a group exercise because it helps people see all at once what can be done and builds group support for follow-through.
No two force fields or problem diagnoses will ever be the same. Every situation is different.	The solution, package, design, policy, or system that works well for someone else may *not* work well for you.

(Source: Charles Weisbord, *Productive Workplaces*)

This paradigm, which encourages organizations to increase employee motivation through participation, self-management, and problem solving, can be implemented for reasons that are entirely selfish. But it is difficult to draw a line between the use of motivational techniques that rely on monetary incentives, such as raises or bonuses, and techniques that use empowerment, workplace democracy, communication, independence in decision making, and self-management, since these also have a large impact on motivation.

We can see evidence of Lewin's ideas at work today in a number of organizations. For example, we worked recently with a Fortune 500 sales company that moved from management control to empowerment and self-directed teams, in which individuals were asked to take greater initiative, solve problems themselves, and support each other in their work. This change resulted in their becoming far more productive, more personally satisfied, and contributing much more to the organization's bottom line.

Former "bean counters" became partners with sales representatives in creating more effective and satisfying contracts with customers. These teams collected money that was owed to the company by customers earlier, with greater accuracy, fewer mistakes, and without leaving large amounts unpaid for months at a time. Team members began to enjoy their work more, and many grew into positions of greater responsibility and leadership within the company.

Paradigm #5: Work Has a Human Side

Lewin's studies focused on industrial democracy and on overcoming resistance to the command and control orientation that had begun with Taylor, rather than on the human element in production. The idea that work has a human dimension began to appear as a paradigm during World War II. In order to identify candidates for the Office of Secret Service, the spy network that preceded the CIA, a more sophisticated psychological testing and placement procedure was developed that focused on the human personality and its reactions to stress.

At the same time, personality studies began to be considered in designing military equipment and industrial machinery for maximum effectiveness. It made no sense for the army to design a tank in which soldiers felt claustrophobic or unable to breathe. After World War II and the Depression, advertising for consumer products opened a new door on personal motivation. Vance Packard's classic book, *The Hidden Persuaders,* and other studies revealed a connection among human needs, personalities and the motivation to buy products that was induced by advertising.

Simultaneously, the tremendous expansion of industry and the need to find appropriate jobs for returning servicemen made employee selection and job placement key issues for managers. The number of companies using psychological tests to select employees for openings grew rapidly from 14 percent at the end of World War II to 75 percent in 1952.

Increasingly during the 1950s, industrial psychologists were criticized for ignoring "human relations" factors, serving only the interests of top corporate management, and using invalid testing procedures, leading to a "human relations revolution" sparked by psychologist Douglas McGregor. The work of McGregor and his colleagues, Abe Maslow, Mason Hare, Dick Beckhard, and Charles K. Ferguson, followed by Warren Bennis and others, was based not only on the theories of Kurt Lewin, but also on the work of Theodoro Adorno, Erich Fromm, and other psychologists who attempted to understand the authoritarian personality that had flourished under fascism. The war against Hitler had increased their resolve to create guarantees against the prejudicial and authoritarian mindset that existed even in American institutions and organizations.

McGregor wrote that classical organizational theory, which he called "Theory X," assumed that employees naturally disliked their work, shunned responsibility, and were not interested in anything beyond job security and wages. Management's role under the Theory X paradigm was authoritarian, top down, and suppressive. On the other hand, McGregor's paradigm, which he called "Theory Y," assumed the opposite for both employees and management. It affirmed the democratic ideals that had been defended and won in the war, and called for an empowered workforce at home. The chart on the next page by McGregor clarifies the distinction between these two paradigms.

You may notice in reading this chart that many differences in management style are a result of fundamentally differing views of human nature, or perhaps it is the other way around, that our views of human nature are simply rationalizations or extensions of the way we treat each other. And it may well be that both of these very different assessments of what is important to people are simply external expressions of how we feel about ourselves.

Throughout our history, we have created workplaces and organizations with purposes that are somehow more important than the people who

Motivating Subordinates

(Two Sets of Assumptions about People)

Traditional (Theory X)	Potential (Theory Y)
1. People are naturally lazy; they prefer to do nothing.	People are naturally active; they set goals and enjoy striving.
2. People work mostly for money and status rewards.	People seek many satisfactions in work: pride in achievement; enjoyment of process; sense of contribution; pleasure in association, stimulation of new challenges, etc.
3. The main force keeping people productive in their work is fear of being demoted or fired.	The main force keeping people productive in their work is the desire to achieve their personal and social goals.
4. People remain children grown larger; they are naturally dependent on leaders.	People normally mature beyond childhood; they aspire to independence, self-fulfillment, and responsibility.
5. People expect and depend on direction from above; they do not want to think for themselves.	People close to the situation see and feel what is needed and are capable of self-direction.
6. People need to be told, shown, and trained in proper methods of work.	People who understand and care about what they are doing can devise and improve their own methods of doing work.
7. People need supervisors who will watch them closely enough to be able to praise good work and reprimand errors.	People need a sense that they are respected as capable of assuming responsibility and self-correction.
8. People have little concern beyond their immediate, material interests.	People seek to give meaning to their lives by identifying with nations, communities, houses of worship, unions, companies, and causes.
9. People need specific instruction on what to do and how to do it; larger policy issues are none of their business.	People need ever-increasing understanding; they need to grasp the meaning of the activities in which they are engaged.
10. People appreciate being treated with courtesy.	People crave genuine respect from other people.

(Source: Douglas McGregor, *The Human Side of Enterprise*)

work in them, workplaces in which we are allowed to be treated as less than human. McGregor's research, and that of his followers, clearly shows that treating people with respect is fundamental to motivating them, and that a little bit of human kindness goes a long way.

Recently a medical unit in a hospital that works with adolescents who are in crisis asked us to help increase its effectiveness in dealing with their teenage clients. The staff members were so preoccupied with responding to emergencies and crises in the lives of the people they treated that they had ignored their own problems. Issues of employee burn-out, sexual harassment, psychological stress, and racial and ethnic tensions were facts of life inside this unit. With the growing demands on the healthcare industry for change and efficiency, these pressures were increasing.

By taking time to pay attention to the human side of their work and stopping to repair the damage they had been doing to themselves, the medical workers learned that they could be much more useful to their clients. As a Friday afternoon ritual, they began giving flowers to one another, which completely changed the culture of the organization. They participated in workshops on how to respond to racial, ethnic, and gender issues. They learned how to understand and prevent sexual harassment. They began to take time to be human with one another.

Paradigm #6: Work Is a Source of Pleasure and a Means of Personal Enjoyment

McGregor's paradigm leads to a post-modern, post-industrial dilemma, but does not answer it. What happens to work when survival is no longer a primary concern? What happens to the work process when motivation is based not simply on increased output, but on artistic freedom, self-actualization, or enjoyment and pleasure? What will happen to work when ridiculous and brute tasks, which constitute most of our work, are finally taken over by computers and robots? Will human labor cease being a commodity and instead become a need? What will people do? How will they survive?

We believe we are beginning to see, in the most technologically advanced societies, an end to the paradigm of the *necessity of work,* of work as drudgery, and the beginning of a paradigm of the *possibility of work,* of work as a source of joy and pleasure; a transition from work-as-means-of-survival to work-as-means-of-fulfillment, work as an essential part of growth, work as self-actualization, and work as personal satisfaction.

Seeing work as a critical element in the creation of relationships, both with ourselves and with others, has the potential of allowing it to become not only a means of creating products, but also a way of creating *ourselves*, as individuals and as members of teams, organizations, communities, and societies.

The paradigm shift we believe we are now beginning to experience is far reaching. It affects not only the way we work, but also how we think about the way we work and the language we use to describe it. This change in the paradigm of work has profound implications for every part of our lives.

The disruptions and conflicts we are now experiencing as a result of mass layoffs; the elimination of whole categories of work; the advances in robotics, telecommuting, outsourcing; the application of computers to many different kinds of tasks; and the other changes highlighted in the previous chapter, indicate that a deep transformation is taking place in the way we work. We believe that this transformation will mean a complete redesign of the entire work process, and perhaps the elimination of workplaces altogether.

Each of the paradigm changes we have seen thus far has built on an earlier paradigm and moved our understanding of the work process toward greater humanity, independence, responsibility, collaboration, and democracy, more than any of the paradigms that existed before it. And each succeeding paradigm has brought us closer to ourselves, to our own true nature, and helped us humanize our workplaces.

In a recent issue of the *New York Times*, Alan Ryan reviewed a book by Richard Wightman Fox about John Dewey's philosophy, which, though developed early in this century, accurately describes the interplay of self and community that is at the heart of this new paradigm:

> [Dewey] held that authentic individual growth always meant a deepening of social engagement. Individual freedom was to be seen not as the negative state of being left alone but as the positive culmination of a calling, an activity that set a person into the web of community. Selfhood was social from start to finish. Society would get the equilibrium it needed when individuals embarked on paths of true self-realization, and those paths had to be made available to everyone through a democratic reordering of work and education.

We believe the new paradigm of work as a source of freedom, fulfillment, and pleasure; as a way of participating in the "web of community;" and as an expression of our need for social interaction and relationship, is only just beginning, and is revealed more and more as we eliminate the old paradigms that saw work as an obligation and a drudgery. At some point in the near future, we will be able to accomplish much of the work we do today by automatic electronic processing. What will motivate us then, if not our own learning and pleasure?

We can see this paradigm beginning to take effect in many employee-empowered organizations. For example, while we were designing a training in self-directed teams, we met a woman we will call Farah, who was a line employee. Farah's co-workers selected her to be interviewed because she was well liked, respected for her work, and considered a "tough cookie" who would tell us the truth about what was happening in the organization. She was skeptical, cynical, disbelieving, and quite articulate. She had been disappointed by too many promises, burned by too many hot new ideas, and was withholding judgment until she saw clear results.

As the team process unfolded, Farah was drawn more and more into designing and implementing the changes that came out of the team-building process. She found she had teamwork and leadership abilities that she had not previously used or valued. Her skill in maintaining an informal communication network became important in developing links between the different teams inside the organization.

Three years into the team-building process, Farah completed a master's degree in psychology, traveling a great distance from her job as a line employee. She looks and acts differently, too. Gone is her perpetual frown and scowl. She trusts herself more and has given up her automatic cynicism as a response to any new proposal. She shows more of herself to the world, and the self she presents is fresh, alive, and excited. Work has become for her a powerful source of personal growth and satisfaction.

Evidence of Past Paradigms Today: An Exercise

As you read this short history of work paradigms, did you notice any that still exist in your organization? The paradigms we identified are relisted below. In the space provided, think of examples of these paradigms that operate in your present work life. Try to be specific, using names of people who exemplify an old paradigm in their behavior, or instances in which you or your colleagues have behaved as if the old paradigm were still true. When you have completed this exercise, share your analysis with others in your organization and compare perceptions. Then ask what you might do to eliminate the use of these old paradigms at work.

Paradigm #1.　Labor is performed by slaves or by disenfranchised workers who can be treated inhumanely

_____

_____

_____

Paradigm #2.　Labor needs to be controlled through scientific management and efficiency

_____

_____

_____

Paradigm #3.　Government has a right to regulate work

_____

_____

_____

Paradigm #4.　Workers are more productive and motivated when self-managed

_____

_____

_____

Paradigm #5.　Work has a human side

_____

_____

_____

Paradigm #6.   Work is a source of pleasure and a means of personal
enjoyment

_____

_____

_____

FOUR

How We Can Humanize the Way We Work

A master in the art of living knows no sharp distinction between his work and his play, his labor and his leisure, his mind and his body, his education and his recreation. He hardly knows which is which. He simply pursues his vision of excellence through whatever he is doing and leaves others to determine whether he is working or playing. To himself he always seems to be doing both.

GEORGE BERNARD SHAW

Key Elements of the New Paradigm

In previous chapters we have argued that we create ourselves through our work; that work can be satisfying and pleasurable; and that humanizing the workplace, both in process and in content, is realistic and possible. We have learned that to transform our organizations we need to change the contexts and paradigms through which we understand our work experience. We have seen what contexts and paradigms are, and looked briefly at the history of some major paradigms operating in the workplace. The question we now face is how an organization operating under the new paradigm would behave. How will we know it when we see it? How will it act? What processes will it use?

It is often the visionary who sees things first. We have known these visionaries in all sizes and shapes:

- A teacher in an urban elementary school who figured out that if she and three of her colleagues combined their classes and each teacher focused on the content she loved the most, the children would learn more and everyone would be motivated to excel.
- A former lineperson at a telephone company who realized that self-directed teams would create an opportunity for her to breathe, to express herself, to shine as a leader, to do more interesting and complex work, and to make a real and permanent contribution to the organization.
- A former house cleaner who once spoke only Spanish and became a teacher, and then the executive director of an early childhood and family center when she realized that unless the community was safe and clean, unless the children rejected gang participation, and unless the families she served discovered nonviolent ways to solve their problems, her work and her life would not be satisfying or effective.
- A president of a large entertainment corporation who understood that employees need to be able to enjoy their work, to be acknowledged for their contributions, and to maintain a family atmosphere while growing rapidly, who took a risk by promoting innovative ways for them to achieve a balanced lifestyle.

We have learned from these inspiring visionaries that a number of core processes or elements define the new paradigm of work and need either to be brought into existence or turned into priorities in order to actually create humanized, participatory, responsible, democratic, and empowered work environments.

We can think of these core elements as shared values, since they reflect the way most of us would like to be treated by others. We can also think of them as ways of making our work lives more congruent with our personal and relational lives. If we uphold the virtue of honesty or openness in our closest personal relationships, why should we not affirm and practice these same values in the workplace?

Humanizing the workplace means making it a place where human values hold sway. Thus, if we say we value honesty, and actually only value profit making or efficiency—sometimes at a substantial human cost—we are not living according to our values. Each of us models through our behavior what we actually value in ourselves and in others. If we are corrupt, if we lie and cheat, if we avoid responsibility and treat others without respect, we are communicating that our behavior is acceptable for others to use as well.

Employees watch their leaders and managers closely for even the slightest signs of inconsistency between what they say and what they actually do. One of our clients was famous for saying he had an open-door policy and wanted to hear from his direct reports at any time about any issue. His second in command told us about the unwritten part of the invitation. If anyone took the boss up on it and dared to tell him what they actually thought, the response was usually so angry, defensive, or forceful that they felt like they were "trying to take a drink from a fire hose."

If we are going to be serious about transforming our workplaces, about humanizing them and making them into sources of pleasure and personal satisfaction, if we are actually going to treat each other humanely, rather than merely as means to material ends, we will need to change not only what we explicitly value, but also how we demonstrate that we actually do value it. Two advocates of change in their organization put it this way:

> I think we all have to take ownership and get past the point of having patience with the finger pointing that goes on. We are all players and need to live by what we say we care about. We will find ourselves in the same system unless all of us decide to take it upon ourselves to do one little thing differently.

> I think everyone has to agree that it is not working and that something needs to change. We need a model that everyone buys into and doesn't shoot down as if they had no part in creating it. They not only have to support it, but enroll others.

What follows is a list of processes, values, behaviors, or core elements that we believe are necessary to humanize the workplace that can serve as guides for how we actually behave. You can use these values as requests to those who are above you in the organizational hierarchy, and as principles for your own behavior, especially in relation to those who work for you. You can also use them to spark a dialogue inside your organization, or between members of your team, over what core values are important to you and need to be acted upon. You can work together to make them real.

Fourteen Values that Make Work a Source of Satisfaction

We have outlined below the 14 values we believe humanized and empowered organizations need, and we have introduced them with examples from our own experience. Can you identify examples from your organization? If these values do not exist or are not acted on in your workplace, your organization may need to create a new paradigm or context, or eliminate some of the old paradigms and contexts we discussed in the last two chapters.

I. INCLUSION

We were once called to a high school that was embroiled in a bitter conflict and asked to help pull the staff back together. Not only were there factions on the staff, but even the factions had factions! We began the session by asking staff members to sit in a circle and introduce themselves. One member of the faculty, Max, sat toward the back, outside the circle, looking like a trouble-making student. We asked him to join the circle and he refused. We asked again and he still wouldn't move. The room was tense, and it appeared we were going to have a power struggle in the first five minutes of the meeting!

Finally we said to him, "Max, we really want to hear what you have to say. The group needs your contribution if it's going to come up with real solutions. If you sit so far away we won't be able to hear you or interact with you." We made it clear through body language and silence that we would not proceed without him. Finally, Max moved his chair. When he participated in the introductory exercise, which was to say one word that described the ideal school, Max's word was *respect*. After we heard from everyone, we asked if anyone objected to any of these words. No one objected. We had gained our first point of consensus, because we had begun the activity with inclusion, using a technique that was inherently respectful. As we went through the session, we repeated Max's word several times as a way of acknowledging his contribution, and he became a full and active participant in the change process.

No one in an organization should be left out of the task of improvement. Everyone has something to contribute. You can find many ways for everyone to be heard without having work grind to a halt and without supporting negative behavior. In the exercise we used with Max, more than 100 people introduced themselves in an activity that took less than half an hour. New methods of inclusion need to be created to embrace all functions, sections, cliques, individuals, groups, and players. Retreats, suggestion boxes, secret ballots, teams, cross-team dialogues, debates, discussions, surveys, conflict audits, departmentwide meetings, open houses, quality circles, employee-run forums, group negotiations, social gatherings and so on, are just a few ways of providing entry into discussion and decision making for each person. Creating these opportunities empowers others and offers encouragement to speak up and participate.

In a school district we have been working with, we facilitated a discussion on how to respond to violent children, as well as those who were "at-risk," and planned strategies with a team that included the classroom teacher, a counselor, a parent, an administrator, and a member of the custodial and cafeteria staff. It turned out that the people who knew most about many of these students were the janitors and cafeteria workers, and they were also often in the best position to have heart-to-heart talks with the students and help them correct their behavior. If these individuals hadn't been included as partners, the group could not have been nearly as successful in reaching students who were in trouble.

2. COLLABORATION

When one of the Baby Bell companies decided to implement self-directed teams for its unionized staff, we were asked to meet with the leadership of the union to discuss the potential of the team model and to sell the idea of teams to the union. However, we met with considerable resistance from the union's leaders. They felt that since management had not included them in the decision to implement self-directed teams, they could not adequately prepare their membership for the shifts in job responsibilities that this approach would entail.

The problem was that the union had been called in *after* the organization had already made its decision to switch to teams. The two union leaders told the company sales managers that the union should have been involved from the beginning of the process, and not be brought in only to give its blessings to a partially implemented program. From the union's perspective, and from ours, true collaboration has to start at the beginning. The project, though of great benefit to the union members, would result in employees doing some managerial jobs on self-directed teams, and the union leaders felt they could not endorse this move without preparing their membership. If management had worked with the union as soon as it started to consider the plan, they could have found a way around this dilemma, but because of the timing of the announcement in relation to collective bargaining, internal union elections, and how it had been communicated to employees, the union's leaders had been put in a bind.

Work today is almost exclusively social, and cannot be accomplished without collaboration, negotiation, give and take, joint problem solving, consensus decision making, conflict resolution, and mutual respect. Collaboration is not the same as compromise. Collaboration is building partnerships from the beginning. It is a joint process of finding and agreeing on solutions by everyone who has a stake in the outcome. Collaboration is an essential skill for teams and networks because it calls forth the best in each individual and allows teams to produce more than any noncollaborating group of employees or managers could possibly deliver.

True collaboration needs to be 100 percent, and needs to include involvement in decision making, sharing information, and joint control over process. John Case, in his breakthrough book, *Open Book Management, The Coming Business Revolution*, argues that collaboration needs to be supported by making all pertinent information—even confidential financial data that is usually kept secret by the organization available to everyone from the CEO to the mailroom staff:

> *In open-book companies people learn to follow the numbers and help make decisions. They learn to think and act like owners, like business-people, and not like hired hands.*

In open-book companies, employees are encouraged to understand every aspect of the company's financial and business condition, including information about performance that is usually only shown to shareholders or top management. Employees receive regular updates so they can see if their performance has generated positive results. Because they have a direct stake in the company's success, they are accountable to one another, rather than to upper management. At Springfield ReManufacturing, author John Case credits this approach with making a failing company highly profitable and creating a huge increase in employee earnings.

Involving everyone and working by consensus is not easy or efficient in the short run, but in the long run it is actually more efficient because it dramatically reduces conflict and resistance. Collaboration is not only a way of getting the job done, it is also a way of improving relationships so the job gets done better the next time. Working well with others is also a source of immense pleasure and satisfaction, and an end in itself.

We were once asked to conduct a training in collaborative negotiation and conflict resolution in preparation for collective bargaining at a medium-sized college with negotiating teams representing the administration and the professors' union. After the training, the teams reached a collective-bargaining agreement, which usually took eight months to negotiate, after only two days! The reason was that they were working together to solve their problems, rather than against each other. These gains carried over to other areas, and people found themselves taking much less time to achieve their goals because they now trusted each other.

3. TEAMS AND NETWORKS

For three years we worked with an information systems organization in a large company that migrated to self-directed teams. In the early stages of team formation, an issue developed over which team had responsibility for providing service to customers with personal computers that were not part of the network system. No team wanted the job, and the director of the unit, Judy, did not want to force a decision. The issue was raised in one of our training sessions with three of the teams that reported to Judy as an example of an unresolved problem that had developed between their teams.

During the training, we asked the teams to meet and plan what they were going to do. They decided to pick representatives from each of their teams to meet with members of the two other teams in Judy's division that were not in the training and come up with a joint plan. The strategy they created is a perfect example of the power of teams and networks. The teams proposed to Judy that they would facilitate her next divisionwide meeting. They created an agenda that they sent to her for approval; used their own facilitator and recorder; brought coffee, donuts, and flip charts; discussed the issues; presented the options and the recommendation of all the teams; and argued in favor of a solution that worked for everyone, especially Judy! After the meeting she called to tell us how thrilled she was that they had taken the initiative and handled it so responsibly.

There is a scale that is appropriate for the accomplishment of every task. Small work teams of four or five people are appropriate for many group tasks, while others require only one or two people, and still others need representatives from a large and diverse constituency. It is important to identify the number of people who are appropriate to the handling of each task, and to use small teams wherever possible because of the ease with which communication flows in small groups. But it is also important to recognize that even large groups can behave like teams if they are organized properly and are given a team focus.

Forcing decision making through multiple levels in a hierarchy only creates traffic jams, communications silos, problem-solving bottlenecks, and a separation between those who know about the problem intimately and those who have the authority to decide how it will be solved. This form of decision making is becoming increasingly obsolete. Teams that are empowered, self-directed, and self-managed are able to replace the need for multiple levels of middle managers and can act both rapidly *and* responsibly. Networks of affiliated teams, organizations, suppliers, customers, and departments are able to integrate design ideas that satisfy multiple sets of interests, increase the quality and quantity of communication flow, transact all aspects of business, buy and sell, hire and fire, and make virtually every kind of decision previously thought to be the exclusive prerogative of upper management.

4. VISION

Recently we were asked to work closely with one of the most exciting and interesting museums in our state. It is undergoing a major transformation with new buildings, new exhibits, new services, and new surroundings. But the internal workings of the organization were still rocky, and several people asked: "How can we complete all these new projects when we can't handle what we're doing now?" The staff felt stressed, demoralized, and unable to communicate with each other. We suggested that everyone—

custodians, security guards, curators, secretaries, executives—be invited to a two-day retreat to redesign the organization from the inside out, that they all participate in a strategic-planning process, and that they try to convince cynical, burned-out steering committee members that the session would allow them to be heard.

We met at a lovely hotel near the beach. Employees were surprised and pleased that they were being treated with such respect and caring, but were still suspicious and questioning. On the first day we asked everyone to join in creating a vision for the future of the institution. The CEO promised that if the group created a vision, it would be valued and would have meaning for the organization as it proceeded through the strategic-planning process.

Creating a vision brought everyone back in touch with why they were there in the first place. They saw clearly that they had dreams and wishes for themselves, their communities, and their families and children. They realized that each of them had something important to contribute. In two hours, the organization had started to come together, and the optimism and energy needed to create themselves anew had been released.

It is essential for all organizations today, public and private, to provide a higher quality of service to the public and be able to respond more rapidly and strategically to ever-changing economic conditions. Customer service, strategic planning, rapidity, and flexibility cannot be maximized without a vision of the purposes and direction of the organization to which everyone is genuinely committed.

We cannot actually create commitment; all we can do is elicit and release it. By inclusion and democratic process; by envisioning and strategic planning; by dialogue and honest, respectful communication; by openness and problem solving; and by negotiation and conflict resolution, we create the possibility for employees to have an impact not only on their work, but also on the overall direction of the entire organization and on the quality of their lives. Their vision then becomes a strong generator of commitment.

Envisioning is a natural, easy process that lends itself to building consensus. Visions can be created on a large scale for 3, 5, 10, or 20 years, for the next six months of a team's work, or for the lifetime of an individual. Visions are like Dumbo's feather; they are an excuse to talk about what really matters. They can be re-created and revised whenever the group needs to return to basics and discover what everyone values individually and collectively.

Several years ago, we helped facilitate a week-long envisioning retreat for IMPACT II with teachers from across the country to create a national teacher's vision for the future of education. Several visions had been drafted for the future of education, but this was the first vision to be created entirely by teachers. As a result of the extraordinary energy and excitement we experienced that week, several teachers returned home and organized envisioning workshops in their own districts. A number of these teachers created visions for their schools, classrooms, families, and students and became leaders, helping others learn how to create visions for their communities and schools.

5. CELEBRATION OF DIVERSITY

Government directives have influenced aerospace companies to pay close attention to issues of gender, race, and ethnic diversity, which led to our being invited to deliver annual workshops on prejudice reduction and bias awareness to more than 1,200 aerospace-research employees. These workshops were designed to give each racial, ethnic, and gender group an opportunity to feel pride in its own identity and culture and to learn more about the experiences of others from different backgrounds.

As part of a storytelling exercise in which each group was asked to describe the experience of growing up as a member of that group, a very dapper African-American engineer spoke of being stopped numerous times by police while he was driving through a wealthy Los Angeles neighborhood and being angrily, repeatedly, and aggressively asked why he was driving there. A slight young African-American man who worked in the mail room told how he felt when he observed caucasian women clutch at their purses when they saw him coming. A female secretary described how she felt when her boss gave her unsolicited shoulder massages as she was typing. A Latina scientist reminisced about how her father would beat her if she spoke Spanish at home because he was determined that she would learn English and "become an American." A group of Asian engineers spoke of the cultural taboos against requesting promotion for themselves. A young gay man described how people at work would hesitate to shake hands with him out of a fear of contracting AIDS.

These anecdotes illustrate the feelings of many employees from diverse backgrounds that they are not accepted for who they are, but judged on the basis of characteristics they were born with and have no control over. A part of humanizing the workplace is making it a place where differences are not seen as threats, but as sources of curiosity, interest, strength, and possibility. Teams flourish under conditions of diversity because differences in culture, perspective, personality, approach, skill, and orientation allow the team to choose among many alternative paths.

Increasingly, and for the foreseeable future, organizations will be meeting grounds for people from very diverse backgrounds. The complexity of the workplace in terms of gender, race, ethnicity, nationality, physical handicap, age, language, sexual orientation, culture, and heritage plays itself out not only in an expanded organizational capacity for growth and change, but also in decision-making styles, communication patterns, personal interactions, expectations for behavior, and leadership skills.

In a participatory work environment, diversity becomes an extraordinary source of richness, vitality, and strength. The challenge for every individual at every level in every workplace and organization is to draw out the potential that lies in each unique human being, to respect the values created by their multicultural and multidimensional backgrounds, and to convert their usual responses from suspicion, distancing, and prejudice to those of curiosity, respect, acceptance, and *celebration* of diversity.

Following the civil unrest in Los Angeles several years ago, we facilitated a series of workshops in prejudice reduction for community organizers who had been hired by the Federal Emergency Management Agency (FEMA) to help people in the community learn how to discuss their cultural and racial differences and work together toward common goals. Groups met in cross-cultural teams and brainstormed ideas for how to bring the community together.

One of the small groups came up with an idea the rest of the group loved. They reported that each member of the group had agreed to invite to his or her home three individuals or couples who represented the other major cultures in Los Angeles. The hosts agreed to ask their guests to bring food, music, and other artifacts that represent their culture, to talk about what they love about their culture, and to agree to invite to their homes the following month three other individuals or couples representing cultures other than their own, thus creating an expanding network of dinner parties to bridge cultural differences.

6. PROCESS AWARENESS

At a large, very hierarchical company where we have worked for several years, one of the employees, Michael, has routinely rolled his eyes and smirked at other people's ideas as a way of controlling the leadership team and making everyone fear his disapproval. He let it be known by "subtle" behavior that there were those he liked and those he didn't. In his heart, he felt he was a good team member and sincerely believed his ideas were right for the organization. On some level, however, he understood the fear he engendered and liked using it to get his way. When we observed the team, we noticed that he usually sat the farthest away from the table, often with an empty chair next to him.

We decided to videotape the team over a period of several weeks. Michael was shocked by the clear message his nonverbal communication was sending. His initial comments were: "Is that really me? How annoying. I wish he'd wipe that sneer off his face!"

The team members also learned a lesson about their willingness to be bullied by him. We taped their meetings, then edited key moments from over 10 hours of footage for the them to review. Some team members were surprised by their own nonverbal actions. They saw themselves lower their eyes or shrink under Michael's glare, move back from the table as he moved forward, and physically acquiesce to his signals. The discussion that followed brought these insights out into the open. The team and Michael agreed that it was OK for them to call him on his behavior, and he apologized for the damaging impact he had had on the group's process.

Michael became aware that his nonverbal communication was just as important as the ideas he communicated to the group. He learned that content and process are not simple dichotomies, but are actually different expressions of the same underlying meaning. It is not sufficient for us, in trying to understand a communication, to address merely the words that are spoken. We have to consider the entire context of the communication, the process by which it is delivered, the means used to express it, and the *relationship* between those who create it.. The meaning of any communication is determined, we believe, by a combination of the following factors:

Meaning:	In the absence of context, and regardless of the words used, what is the meaning of what is being communicated?
Intention:	What affect on the listener was intended by the speaker?
Awareness:	What level of awareness of the communication is present in the listener?
Understanding:	How much of what is being communicated does the listener understand?
Acceptance:	Which parts of the communication are acceptable to the listener and which are not?
Process:	How was the message communicated? What was the tone? What was the energy level?

Context:	What is the context, structure, or system within which the communication is made? How does it affect the meaning of the communication?
Relationship:	What is the relationship between the speaker and the listener? What is their history? What do they expect from each other in the future?

Team process is concerned not just with communication, but with other process skills as well, such as facilitation, problem solving, negotiation, and conflict resolution. Process skills are as important in producing results as the technical skills required to complete the project. In the future workplace, a knowledge of how people interact with one another, a subtle awareness of listening styles, an ability to work collaboratively, a knowledge of techniques for reaching consensus, and an understanding of group dynamics will be considered essential skills and requirements for success.

We frequently encounter organizations in which communication has broken down and been replaced by growing distrust, reliance on authoritarian figures or processes, isolation, resistance, deteriorating morale, and *chronic* conflict. Our experience is that simply meeting together to talk about these problems, using a process that is inclusive, collaborative, open, honest, and democratic often solves the problem automatically.

We recently facilitated a problem-solving retreat for a large government agency that was experiencing serious morale problems. We asked everyone to meet in small groups to identify all the problems that were causing their morale to suffer. When the staff read off their lists, which were long and depressing, we asked each of the groups if they had experienced any of these problems or difficulties while they met. None of the groups had experienced any of the problems in their efforts to complete the exercise. We then asked why they hadn't, since they had listed so many serious problems, and at least one or two ought to have shown up in their groups. It quickly became clear to the staff that their problems were a result of their process, and when they worked together as a team, their morale lifted and they were able to work together much more effectively.

7. OPEN AND HONEST COMMUNICATION

There is an apocryphal story about Samuel Goldwyn, who once remarked: "I don't want any 'yes men' in my organization. I want each person to speak his mind, even if it does cost them their job." One of the school districts we worked with was moving to a "360-degree" evaluation process that is becoming popular in many organizational settings. This new evaluation process eliminates top-down assessments of employee performance based solely on the rating of a single supervisor and substitutes a multifaceted performance evaluation that is completed by the employee, his or her peers or team members, managers, direct reports, and "customers" or clients. Everyone assesses everyone else. The following chart illustrates this process.

360-Degree Evaluation

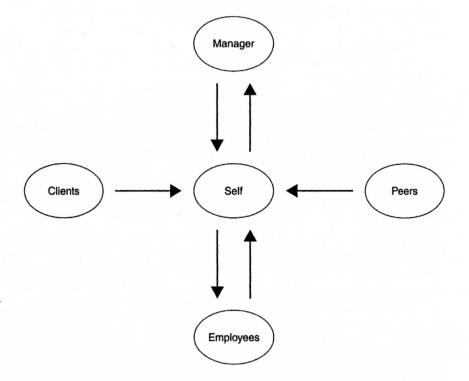

The superintendent of this school district was concerned that his staff would not believe the process was authentic, and would be suspicious of his desire that everyone communicate honestly and openly, not only during the performance appraisal process, but in their regular interactions with one another. So he started the appraisal process by asking for direct and honest feedback on his own performance from all the parents, teachers, administrators, staff, students, and board members in the district. He reported honestly on the results of the evaluation and on his intentions to improve the level of his skills during a districtwide meeting. He thanked everyone, especially those who had taken the greatest risks. He effectively modeled his belief in the new behaviors he wanted to encourage and demonstrated openness, honesty, and risk taking by starting with himself, leaving no room for suspicion or resistance.

We know that information is a tremendous source of power, and that the information we hoard and the secrets we keep distort our relationships and make us less than completely honest; yet most organizations today operate on the basis of secrecy and restrict information to those who "need to know." By doing so, they create a culture in which people gossip instead of communicating directly; in which rumors proliferate and it is safer to hide the truth, particularly if it is unpleasant. In the process, the entire organization is cheated out of learning and improving or correcting the problem.

We encourage organizations to operate on the principle of complete openness and honesty, and to make efforts to train those who will receive the information in how to communicate it skillfully. Nothing is more devastating to an organization than information that is revealed too little or too late, and a great deal can be gained by making our organizations more public. Rather than assume the need for secrecy, we should assume the desire for openness and honesty and require substantial justification before departing from it.

It is common in most organizations for employees to adopt this attitude of secrecy with one another, to gossip instead of being open, and to rely on rumors instead of honest, direct communication. When we encounter an organization that seems to thrive on gossip, we often discover that the people who are leading the organization are hiding information unnecessarily, or giving false information instead of telling the entire truth.

Organizations can always find some good and substantial reason for being duplicious, but these reasons ignore the most important and telling reason for openness and honesty: if you are not honest yourself, you authorize others not to be, and thereby create a culture in which people hide from the truth, are secretive, and disguise their problems so they can't be solved.

Our friend Susan Griffin has written an extraordinary book, *A Chorus of Stones*, which outlines some of the disastrous effects of secrecy in public and private life. She writes:

During my childhood the absence left by all the secrets my parents and the other adults kept from children was numinous and hot. There was the war that had just occurred and, beneath these images of heroism, unspeakable whispered horrors. There was my mother's drinking, just like her father's before her, the flashing sight of her wild laughter and then rage, before my father pulled her out of the hallway and into the privacy of their bedroom. The secret process of atomic fission, the secret mechanism of missiles. All these secrets migrated into one space in my imagination, a geography of lost and missing pieces.

She writes not only about the ways secrets distort our lives and trap us, but also about our need for honest and open communication as the way out of this dilemma:

The stories we tell ourselves, particularly the silent or barely audible ones, are very powerful. They become invisible enclosures. Rooms with no air. One must open the window to see further, the door of possibility.

8. RISK TAKING

Large government agencies rarely support openness and honesty or encourage their employees to take risks. Bureaucracies of all kinds seem to deaden the vitality that is required to risk exposure or try something out of the ordinary. A "mediocracy" sets in, and no one dares to stand out as a maverick. As a result, they encourage little learning, few innovations, and rare bursts of creativity.

Edgar, a long-term client, had been the head of a county service department for more than 15 years. He ran a tight ship, was quite formal with his direct reports and staff, and was seen as a fairly authoritarian manager. He began to realize he had to make some changes in his department in order to increase his staff's ability to be customer oriented, reduce its response time, and create more effective solutions to fit a new set of client requirements. The specter of outsourcing loomed large on the horizon.

We knew we had to begin at the top if all 1,100 of the department's staff members were going to change, so we organized a series of sessions with the leaders of the department to open their communication, increase their ability to work together as a team, and enable them to provide leadership for the changes the department needed to make. The first thing the group members felt they had to do was to confront Edgar, their leader. His style had to change. He had to loosen his iron grip on them and on the department.

We conducted an exercise in which the participants filled out a questionnaire asking them to identify the names of team members in statements denoting greater levels of intimacy and trust. For example, "I would lend my car to _____. I would trust _____ to replace me in my job for a week. I would trust my life with _____." We then asked for a volunteer in the group to share his or her answers. There was a very long, heavy silence, and finally Edgar said, "Well, I guess I'll start." He took a risk by going beyond his comfort level and modeled a new kind of behavior. His risk taking cracked the group wide open. Everyone shared their lists and talked at length about the kind of relationships they wanted and needed to have with each other. It was the beginning of the new organization, and of Edgar's transition from being a manager to being a leader.

Without people who are willing to take risks, make leaps of faith, and experience the failures we learn from, growth cannot occur. The exhilaration that comes from learning to ski or climb a mountain cannot be fully savored until we have eliminated the safety net. We do not find creative answers to our problems by traveling on familiar roads. Mistakes, wrong turns, and failures are all a part of the process of learning and changing. John Cleese of Monty Python fame put it well in a *Fortune* magazine article about risks and failure:

> It's self-evident that if we can't take the risk of saying or doing something wrong, our creativity goes right out the window. . . .The essence of creativity is not the possession of some special talent, it is much more the ability to play.
>
> . . .In organizations where mistakes are not allowed, you get two types of counterproductive behavior. First, since mistakes are 'bad' if they're committed by the people at the top, people can pretend that no mistake has been made. So it doesn't get fixed. Second, if they're committed by people lower down in the organization, mistakes get concealed.

If new ideas are to be explored and innovation is to be encouraged, risk taking and permission for failure need to be not merely allowed, but requested, modeled, acknowledged, supported, rewarded, and celebrated.

9. INDIVIDUAL AND TEAM OWNERSHIP OF RESULTS

In a new self-directed team environment we helped create in a large public service organization, we found some individuals who had been long-term "nonperformers" who were trying to hide in the deepest recesses of the team process. On some teams, members were unsure about how to address the problem of everyone pulling his or her own weight, of owning the job, and being responsible for results.

Teri, one of the people who had been getting the job done, grew frustrated with the "slackers" on her own team and on the teams with which she interfaced. In graduate school, she had been researching the loss of individual responsibility that sometimes occurs on teams. We encouraged her to bring her findings to her team and talk about what happens when individuals relinquish their responsibilities. This report kicked off a discussion on the team about who was responsible for what, which led to an accountability tracking system that was computerized so everyone on the team could monitor how every other person was doing in managing their projects. Those who needed help could then ask for it. Those who were hiding were now out in the open. One member of the team who couldn't tolerate the scrutiny finally left the organization. But the group became a true team of mutually supporting, fully responsible players.

Team behavior can often look like "group think" in which no one is accountable and everyone defers to the nameless, faceless control of the group. However, improved performance and successful teams require that each individual in the group take personal responsibility for all of the team's outcomes, and for the outcomes of other team members as well, without blaming or finger-pointing, which only reduces the ability to learn from failure.

It is only when we stop trying to shift responsibility to someone else and take personal ownership of everything that happens in the organization, including work that is someone else's primary responsibility, that we become committed to finding solutions to problems that otherwise block us from achieving high performance results, and that we realize that we have an obligation to speak out and disagree if we don't think the job is being done right.

Not only does the individual need to speak out and take responsibility for the work of the team, the team needs to support and be responsible for the work of the individual, encouraging team members to raise criticisms and problems, helping out when there is a need, cross-training, and providing backup and honest feedback so that each person can achieve his or her highest potential.

We worked with a team of teachers who were having serious problems with one of its members, Ted, who just wanted to do his own individual work and not participate in the team's efforts to solve problems. At one point, Ted was called from a team meeting by the principal to meet with an irate parent over something that had happened in his classroom. When he told the other team members he had to leave, they said, "No you don't. We're going with you to stand by you." Ted was so deeply moved by their willingness to take responsibility for his problems that he became an active and enthusiastic member of the team.

10. PARADOXICAL PROBLEM SOLVING

One of our most unusual assignments was to facilitate an intensive three-day planning process for a world-renowned science museum that wanted to create a national teacher-education center. The task was unusual because the center did not want a linear, final plan as an outcome. Rather, the organization asked that the process capture and preserve the paradoxes, dissimilarities, conflicts, and the wide variety of contradictory ideas that would be generated by a diverse collection of staff, science teachers, and international representatives of the science, political, and education communities who would be invited to the session and critique the ideas.

To solve the problem of how to design a teacher-training center and organize its programs, the museum's manager wanted to hold on to all their open questions, to list the main paradoxes and dissimilarities, and to preserve all the richness and complexity of their uncertainty. The "charette" planning process we facilitated produced several prototypes that were lived with, discussed, and reviewed. The group used these models as sources for a final design workshop from which they created an ultimate plan. This plan was also left open so the center could evolve organically at its own pace, shifting between the four models that were generated during the charette. The paradox of moving in four directions at once created a more powerful program than coming to a single path through a linear process.

In the modern workplace, genuine problem solving is rarely linear. Everyone lives with paradoxes everyday. The natural complexity of the problems we are facing should not be simplified, but explored for information about novel ways of improving the quality of our solutions. Paradox means living simultaneously with two apparently contradictory realities, and the acceptance of parodox is a high value for people working in complex, living organizations.

Ambiguity, paradox, and enigma do not always need to have a solution, but can be thought of as things to be savored and plumbed for the rich range of alternatives they reveal. A time may come to choose a single solution and to act, but before we reach closure, we need to experience fully the complexity and paradox that *actually* exists in the problem, without fearing the contradiction that is expressed in our holding two opposite thoughts at the same time. Umberto Eco expressed our view of paradox and enigma well in his book, *Foucualt's Pendulum:*

> [In the beginning] I believed that the source of enigma was stupidity. Then . . .
> I decided that the most terrible enigmas are those that mask themselves as madness.
> But now I have come to believe that the whole world is an enigma, a harmless
> enigma that is made terrible by our own mad attempt to interpret it as though it
> had an underlying truth.

11. EVERYONE IS A LEADER

When we work with organizations, we know we will eventually leave and not have to live with the results of our consultations and trainings, but our clients will. We therefore try to build internal capacities and skills within the organization, and to leave behind teams of employee leaders who will carry forward the plans and actions they have developed through our work. We hope they will provide coaching and support to others who are also struggling to implement change. Quite often these teams volunteer from the rank-and-file in the company, and new faces begin to emerge in the leadership circle.

As we drew to the end of a year-and-a-half-long relationship with a national accounting organization, we had the pleasure of working with a team of internal trainers and coaches who owned the self-directed team concept and were committed to carrying it forward. The process had worked so well that this team sparked excitement and energy for themselves and among their colleagues.

In our sessions with these trainers, the team learned the basics of delivering a training program in self-directed teams to new employees. They were videotaped and critiqued, they presented a series of mini-trainings to each other, and they jointly coached one another in improving their facilitation and training skills. We then asked the group members if they would like to "take their show on the road."

After some discussion, they came up with the idea of creating a "team university" for their annual all-staff meeting. This idea immediately expanded to include the creation of a "catalog" of the courses they would teach, together with team diplomas, yearbooks, funny awards, caps and gowns for graduation, and so on. We were told the "team university" was a fabulous success. We weren't there, had nothing to do with it, and could only marvel at the extraordinary burst of creativity, ingenuity, and initiative shown by this team of leaders, most of whom had been buried in the accounting department of this large corporation for years.

Leadership is not something that belongs only to those at the head of the organization. We believe it is an obligation on the part of everyone. Leadership means taking charge of your own life and helping others. It means modeling the behavior you advocate and walking your talk. It means reaching out to people wherever they are and helping them, step by step, become and achieve more than they think they are capable of, and it means doing the same with your own life.

People are the leaders in their own lives, whether they realize it or not. As Warren Bennis and Joan Goldsmith wrote in *Learning to Lead: A Workbook on Becoming a Leader:*

> . . .*[we are talking about] leadership, but not leadership with a capital L. The problems are too complex, many layered, numerous and widespread for a small group of "leaders" to have an impact. The problems of our cities require leaders on every block, in every church, in every community. The crisis in education calls for every parent, teacher, classroom aide, student, and administrator to create visions, to inspire commitment, to foster creativity, and to stimulate achievement. The failures in our corporations demand leadership qualities in every staff member, secretary, salesperson, accounts payable clerk, and CEO to catalyze enthusiasm, to encourage risk taking, and to create breakthroughs in innovation. The future will only work if each of us makes it work.*

12. PERSONAL GROWTH AND SATISFACTION

We have been privileged to witness the blossoming of extraordinary qualities in what otherwise might be thought of as very ordinary people, as their work was reshaped to give them greater satisfaction and pleasure.

Here is a typical comment that reveals the level of personal growth that is possible when people move into a team environment:

> My staff is great. Everyone works really hard and they have become smart in every area, and people jump in to help each other. We have begun to develop systems to handle problems proactively. This is exciting, and we are getting good feedback from other divisions appreciating our work. We try to say yes whenever we can. We love being here and we pass it along.

People *do* pass their excitement along when they feel fulfilled, and this feeling starts to pervade the organization. We saw this happen dramatically with one of our most exciting clients who became a good friend in the process of our working together. She headed an information services department in a very large corporation. Her style was to be a powerhouse of creativity, energy, inspiration, and brilliance. But she was trying to create a new organization inside a parent company that had not changed for many years, and was not interested in changing. She was constantly hindered, blocked, questioned, nit-picked, restricted, and frustrated by resistance from her supervisor at every turn. She suffered, her family suffered, and her health suffered, yet she plowed ahead with what she knew was right for her organization.

Finally, when she felt she had established a new structure that was secure, she was offered a new position with a large entrepreneurial conglomerate as chief information officer reporting directly to the CEO. The new company valued and respected her opinion. She proposed candidates she wanted to hire to her boss, who responded "Why are you asking me? If you want them, go get them." She began to flower. She could actually do what was needed and shape the organization to deliver. She was able to create an environment in which people felt valued and empowered. Her family dynamic shifted from internal warfare to a love fest, and her health improved. She was able to begin to consider her inner spiritual life and her long neglected personal growth. The transformation was extraordinary!

In the new work environment that we envision, we will all be able to consciously invent ourselves. Our lives are designed and shaped creatively by and through our work. Cross-training enhances our skills, and flexible schedules and assignments based on initiative support our growth and personal enjoyment. Teams provide us with ways to feel satisfied and useful on the job, to have fun with one another, and to fulfill our responsibilities. Leadership roles in teams give us opportunities to grow because they emerge naturally from our tasks, and a chance to volunteer for roles we never thought we could play. We start to seek out new career opportunities we once thought were beyond our reach and to appreciate that we can be whole people on the job, rather than cogs in a grinding machine. Humanizing the way we work really means that we are allowed to be human beings at work, and to feel that we are entitled to satisfy our needs and desires.

13. Seeing Conflict as an Opportunity

Every conflict is an opportunity for learning, growth, change, improvement, better and more intimate relationships with others, and deeper understanding of ourselves. One of our clients, a teachers' union with many different racial, ethnic, and cultural constituencies faced a difficulty in the possible layoff of social service providers based not on their seniority, but on their ability to speak a second language. This administrative decision pitted African-American and Anglo employees against Latino and Asian-Pacific employees, with all sides vying to influence the union leadership in support of their own group and against the others.

In a group-conflict resolution session, we asked everyone to say what he or she thought the real problem was. Each side started by seeing the other side as the problem, but gradually everyone began to see that the underlying problem was a layoff that seemed designed to set them against one another. By accumulating points of consensus and working closely with each other, these employees were able to develop a number of proposals for action that did not divide them based on their race ethnicity. By engaging in an open dialogue over their conflict, opportunities for unified action emerged that hadn't existed before.

Sparks fly and conflict fills the air every time a new paradigm is created. When we encourage self-direction, increase personal interaction between teams and networks, open up communication and problem solving, negotiate boundaries, make decisions based on consensus, and substitute collaborative for autocratic styles of management, conflicts that had previously been swept under the rug naturally rise to the surface.

We need to see these conflicts as healthy, and as opportunities for organizational growth and learning. Advanced conflict-resolution techniques allow deep organizational problems to be surfaced, aired, resolved, and let go of in a constructive way, while conflict-resolution systems are designed to proactively prevent, channel, and defuse destructive conflicts before they result in serious damage. While the job isn't always easy or efficient, there is a payoff, as described by one of the managers in our trainings:

We should start thinking in terms of strategies for consensus rather than force something to happen. It takes longer, it is messier, it involves walking around, but in the long run there is a bigger payoff.

Many organizations are using a wide range of new techniques from informal problem solving to peer mediation, executive advisers, review boards, ombudsmen, peer counseling, dialogue groups, arbitration, and other alternative dispute resolution processes as part of an effort to reduce the level of unresolved conflict and encourage prevention through the building of collaborative relationships. These techniques are discussed in detail in Section 7.

We worked with a Fortune 100 technology company to help it design an employee problem-resolution procedure that allowed employees to choose from a large number of different options to resolve their problems. They began the process with informal problem solving by the manager, intervention by the human resources department, feedback, and some informal negotiation. Then the dispute went to peer mediation and coaching; from there to an ombudsman, an executive advisor, and an outside mediator; then to an internal review board; and finally to binding arbitration. While this approach may seem time consuming, the company actually saved millions of dollars in attorney's fees and legal costs by using this process.

14. EMBRACING CHANGE

We began a strategic planning process for one of the premier alternative institutions of higher education in the country, Cambridge College, which serves a diverse, nontraditional student body consisting mostly of working adults, and people of color who are midcareer professionals. The college faced a number of complex pressures, which included the shifting priorities of the federal government and an increased demand for baccalaureate and master degree programs by their students. The strengths the college applied to meeting these demands included the commitment of its faculty and administration to excellence, its willingness to continually reexamine the way it delivered services, and its commitment to make far-reaching changes where necessary, which is rare among colleges and universities where tradition often holds sway. One employee of the college made the following statement during our interviews, which illustrates the college's willingness to embrace change:

We should constantly reexamine our academic leadership for the college to assess if we are delivering what is needed by our students. We need to recognize what our strengths are and find ways of sharing them. We have a vision and a mission, but these terms need to be looked at again and again to see whether there are other values in what we do and whether they need updating. We should be sitting at the educational leadership table nationally, helping to make policy changes.

Over a period of a year, we worked with the college to create a process in which every member of the faculty, board of trustees, staff, and administration, from the receptionist to the president, participated in developing ideas for improving the college and giving input into the strategic planning process. Planning committees and task forces were formed, including board members, faculty, administration, and staff, in order to provide leadership to the change process, reassess the college's accomplishments, and develop a concrete plan to improve quality thoughout the institution.

In *Thriving on Chaos* Tom Peters calls for a management revolution that will turn American industry upside down. Peters believes that constant, continual, rapid, and accelerating change is a way of life in the future workplace. There are no blueprints, no charts, no tales from travelers who have been there before. Jobs that existed for life are now temporary. Communication that once took days now happens instantaneously. Structures that were accepted as the norm can be revised at any time and may shift from centralized to decentralized and back again in a year. Visions and missions are reworked on an ongoing basis. Products come and go as fads dictate. There is only experimentation, risk taking, and change, all of which focus on discovering what works, what produces results, and what is most satisfying. And there is no end in sight.

Working to maximize these 14 elements in your organization will help you create your own paradigm shift and develop a more humanized workplace. All of the elements we have reviewed are interrelated; none of them stands alone. If you change one, you change them all, because each one affects the entire organizational system. The exercise that follows will give you an opportunity to apply the elements we have described to your own organization.

Organizational Review: An Exercise

Take some time to reflect on your own organization in light of the elements described above. What examples can you find for each of these areas? Do you find that you are implementing these elements, or that you are suffering by not having them in place? In your own mind, skim through your day-to-day life experiences on the job. Next, rate your work organization on each of the elements listed below. You may want to complete this evaluation on your own and then share it with others, or you may want to do it as a group, discussing each element and comparing notes.

On a scale from 1 to 5 with 1=not valued or evident, 2=rarely valued or evident, 3=sometimes valued and evident, 4=usually valued and evident, 5=always valued and evident, give your organization a score based on the evidence of these elements and how they are valued:

Elements of an Empowered Workplace

1. Inclusion. ___
2. Collaboration. ___
3. Teams and networks. ___
4. Vision. ___
5. Celebration of diversity. ___
6. Process awareness. ___
7. Open and honest communication. ___
8. Risk taking. ___
9. Individual and team ownership of results. ___
10. Paradoxical problem solving. ___
11. Everyone is a leader. ___
12. Personal growth and satisfaction. ___
13. Seeing conflict as an opportunity. ___
14. Embracing change. ___

Once you have scored each element, notice any that you felt deserved a score of three or below. The elements that you scored three or below will require special focus as you try to create a new paradigm. If you are part of a team at work or are participating in a training program, university course, or group discussion, share your ratings with your colleagues. If you are completing this assessment with others from your organization, discuss any discrepancies you notice in how you scored each element and consider how you would answer the following questions.

Questions for the Group to Consider

1. Can you reach consensus on a rating for each element? If not, what is blocking you?
2. Does your perspective on this new paradigm differ based on the level of your position in the organization?
3. Do members of different departments or teams have differing points of view or commitment to the new paradigm?
4. If there is agreement on which elements need the greatest focus, can you think of some steps you might take to increase the organization's commitment to the new paradigm by working on these elements? What are these steps? Write them down in the space below and show them to others.

_____

_____

_____

_____

_____

FIVE

Reinventing the Wheel

Work is love made visible. And if you cannot work with love but only
with distaste, it is better that you should leave your work and sit at the
gate of the temple and take alms from those who work with joy.

KAHLIL GIBRAN

If we are going to genuinely
humanize our workplaces and contour them to the new contexts and
emerging paradigms we describe in previous chapters, we will have to
begin behaving differently toward one another. Yet it is difficult for us to
behave differently when we are surrounded by organizational structures,
cultures, and systems that were designed for the purpose of reinforcing
the old paradigms and contexts.

Here we face one of the paradoxes of change. We need to
fundamentally transform the way we work, our values, systems, structures,
and processes. But how do we transform the way we work without also
reinventing ourselves, without transforming our ways of thinking and
behaving? And how do we transform these ways of thinking and behaving
when they are reinforced by the very values, systems, structures, and
processes that we are trying to change, and are based on old contexts and
paradigms? How do we rethink the organization of our workplaces,
which we have accepted for many years, and at the same time reorganize
the way we rethink them?

In the next three chapters we will lead you through a process that will
help you "reinvent the wheel," and start to restructure the way you think
about your work. We will encourage you to look creatively at some of the
questions whose answers define the systems and structures that affect the
way you work. We will help clarify and define the changes you may want
to make in your workplace and outline the steps you will need to take to
transform your organization. Finally, we will look at alternative ways of
understanding and resolving conflict that always forms a part of the
change process, and search for ways of using conflict as an opportunity
for changing, learning, and humanizing the way we act when we are under
pressure.

We want to suggest two guidelines for beginning the process of
rethinking your organizational system: Start from scratch, and think of
your organization as a system, as a whole.

Start from Scratch

Most of us approach the change process not with open minds, but with a
set of unexamined experiences and assumptions about what needs to

change, how it should be changed, and what should replace it. We often fail to see that these experiences and assumptions have their origins in an old context or paradigm, and either support or recreate it.

We need to start with a blank slate about what it means to organize a group of people to engage in any kind of work. We need to ask ourselves, if we were to build a work organization from scratch, what would be the essential elements that, regardless of history, ideology, form of ownership, culture, national character, product, or area of concentration, would constitute the work relationship.

For example, the highly successful Mondragon Cooperatives in the Basque region of Spain began by bringing workers together to build their relationships and get to know one another months before they decided what products they would produce or how they would structure their organization. They recognized that work is, after all, a relationship, not only with raw materials and finished products, but also with other workers, suppliers, and customers.

Changing a Part Means Changing the System as a Whole

A useful tool in implementing change is to think of organizations as *systems*, as wholes that consist of separate parts yet are also more than simply the sum of these parts. Our efforts to shift our corporations, schools, social service agencies, community organizations, and nonprofit groups to a more humanized, team-based, collaborative, and democratic paradigm led us to examine the need for transformation in all aspects of our lives at work. Similarly, we have found that when our clients attempted to change one part of their organizational system, the other parts seemed to conspire against the change becoming effective. For example:

- A company we worked with began organizing self-directed teams and found it had to alter its compensation system in order to reward and motivate team efforts, as well as individual contributions.
- A school instituted team teaching, and the schedule had to be changed so the team could meet and plan together; curriculum materials had to be revised to integrate math, science, social studies, and language arts; and playground activities needed to be

restructured to allow for multiple classes on the playing field at the same time.

♦ Senior executives instituted a new sexual harassment policy and found they had to train managers in how to listen and respond to complaints of sexual harassment. They had to set up informal problem-solving teams to help resolve the "gray areas" in employee complaints, and they had to hire an ombudsman to investigate and resolve sexual harassment complaints.

♦ A museum launched a strategic planning process to shift the internal culture of the institution and found it had to listen to custodians' concerns about safety, involve secretaries in deciding how work was processed, and invite participation from all levels in the organization to help the staff reorient itself to the new culture.

Every organization is a system of interrelated parts, functions, elements and, most of all, *people*. As you reflect on ways the new contexts and paradigms we have described might apply to your workplace, notice the implications that changing any element in your organization has for all the others. Every part of our working lives operates within a system, and creates that system through its intersection with all the other parts. Changing part of a system means changing the system as a whole, and when the entire organization changes, the meaning and usefulness of each of its parts is altered.

The problem with making small, cosmetic changes in any organization is that the other parts of the system conspire to constrict the change and prevent it from impacting anything fundamental. Sometimes, in order to create even small changes, it is necessary to transform the system as a whole. And sometimes it is necessary to start with small, seemingly insignificant changes that end up having an enormous impact on the system as a whole.

The System of Work

We believe that any work relationship that involves more than one person must perform the following tasks, which, in combination, largely determine how our work is performed, whether the work is managed by teams or by managers, government, employee owners, shareholders, or some combination.

1. *Hiring.* Identify the skills that are needed to produce a desired set of results and hire the individuals who seem to be most skillful at performing them.
2. *Delineation of tasks.* Create a division of labor in order to increase specialization, skill, productivity, and efficiency.
3. *Compensation.* Establish a system (or systems) of compensation for work that is being performed.
4. *Assignment of work.* Organize tasks so that workers can move from one location or job to another as needs change and as they increase their skills.
5. *Training.* Create opportunities for learning so employees can develop and improve their skills and organizations can adapt to changing conditions.
6. *Policies and procedures.* Develop a set of expectations, policies, rules, and relationships, spoken or unspoken, that allow employees and managers to operate efficiently.
7. *Feedback and evaluation.* Evaluate the work that has been done, provide feedback, and correct mistakes.
8. *Motivation.* Establish rewards, punishments, and disciplines that allow organizations to transfer, promote, discipline, or terminate employees where necessary.
9. *Conflict resolution.* Create mechanisms and procedures for finally resolving interpersonal and organizational disputes.
10. *Allocation of deficits and surpluses.* Establish criteria for allocating profits and losses.

These systems or functions are the primary elements that define a modern workplace. The nature of each, how they interact, how successfully they perform, and how they impact the quality of relationships between employees, depends on how effectively, efficiently, and humanely the organization carries out these functions.

Fundamental Decisions: An Exercise

We have posed the questions that follow to raise the practical implications that are involved in shifting to a new context or paradigm. The questionnaire that follows has several possible uses. You may want to answer the questions yourself and compare them with others' answers. Or you may want to create your own written questionnaire, distribute it to your colleagues, tabulate the results, and share them at a staff discussion to elucidate the different points of view you have uncovered. You may also see these questions as a way of providing support for a staff retreat or strategic planning process in which you will be looking for new answers and trying to reach consensus on a set of goals that will move you in a new direction. If your colleagues give different answers to these questions, discuss them, talk them through, and try to come to consensus on where you are and where you need to go. Please base your answers on how you think the questions should be answered, rather than on how your organization presently answers them.

I. Who should make the decision to hire and on what basis?

_____

_____

_____

2. How should compensation be determined?

_____

_____

_____

3. Who should select the managers and how should they manage?

_____

_____

_____

4. Who should get promoted, how, and by what criteria?

_____

_____

_____

5. Who should allocate work and assign tasks, and how are they done?

_____

_____

_____

6. Who should get educated and in what?

_____

_____

_____

7. How should work be evaluated and improved?

_____

_____

_____

8. Who should make and enforce rules, and how effective can the rules be in practice?

_____

_____

_____

9. Who should deal with conflicts, and how can they be resolved?

_____

_____

_____

10. How can profits and losses be divided?

_____

_____

_____

Now go back over these questions and ask yourself whether you prefer any of the answers you gave to your organization's current practices. Did you come up with creative, unorthodox answers that differ from your present reality? How did others react to these ideas? How far out on a limb were you or your colleagues willing to go? We want to continue challenging your assumptions, biases, and preconceptions, both about your answers to these questions, and more importantly, to what answers are possible.

Different answers to any of these questions will produce *vastly* different results in morale and motivation, participation in decision making, and responsibility for results in your organization. They will also result in qualitatively different relationships among employees, managers, executives, customers, the community, and the public. And most importantly, they are the keys to humanizing the workplace.

We asked a group of middle managers in a large manufacturing firm to answer these questions. After they described their ideal organization, we asked them to come to consensus on a description of how their workplace currently operates. The group members needed three meetings to agree on a description of the way they really operate. We next asked them, "How pleased are you with this description?" Finally we asked them, "What would you like to change in your organization?" The answers varied widely, depending on the question and the responder. The conversation that ensued as they struggled for consensus was tremendously useful as a starting point in identifying the changes they wanted to make, the decisions they had to reach, and who was going to participate in making them. Try this in your own group, and when you do, encourage your colleagues to look carefully at how they actually interact.

Implementing the New Paradigm

The following sections give our answers to the questions we posed above based on the new contexts and paradigms we have described. Please think of them as an exploration of alternative ways we can think about work, and as proposals rather than final answers. How each organization answers these questions will necessarily differ based on its mission, the needs of the people who work there, and other elements in the organizational system. Our answers summarize what we have discovered looking at a large number of very different organizations over many years.

I. Who Makes the Decision to Hire and on What Basis?

Employees can be seen to exist solely to serve the interests of managers and owners in an organization, or management can be seen to serve the interests of employees, with multiple gradations in-between. We have seen the central administrative office of a school district rename itself "The Service Center," and adopt an upside-down pyramid as its organizational chart to give symbolic recognition to the idea that its function is to serve the students, teachers, staff, and families who are at the top of the hierarchy.

Employees and managers may relate to each other in two fundamentally different ways, which are reflected throughout the organization. They can either relate autocratically or democratically; based on command or initiative; in hierarchies or in teams; with or without responsibility for results; motivated negatively or positively. These choices are made initially in the way employees are hired.

The decision to hire can be made unilaterally by management based on criteria it alone has selected, jointly with staff, unilaterally by employees, or by self-directed teams. In most enterprises today, management selects the people who are hired, largely without input, veto authority, or much consultation from the people who actively perform the work in question.

Purely on the basis of productivity and efficiency, the advantages of staff members hiring other staff members are many:

- They are usually better qualified to choose their co-workers than managers, who do not perform their particular work on a regular basis.
- By making the selection, responsibility for results shifts to those who will make certain there is appropriate training and supervision.
- Poor performers are less likely to think they can escape detection or get away with slack performance when the employees who hired them are watching and depending on them.
- Employees who are hired by a team feel a greater obligation to support their peers and team members and perform at a higher level than for someone who is above them in power.
- Errors are likely to be corrected more quickly, and poor performers may be disciplined and replaced with less opposition

and resistance from other employees, who will not be as worried for their own job security as when management alone makes these decisions.

The reasons for using the less effective method of having managers do the hiring is based more on status and a desire to maintain the power, control, and authority of management than on selecting the best qualified person to do the job.

One of our most successful consulting engagements began with our being interviewed and hired by a staff team, none of whom was a manager. Team members screened all the candidates for the consultancy, negotiated the contract, hired us, monitored the results we produced, and worked with us as a support team to guarantee our success. Part of the reason we were successful was that the employees felt they had hired us, and we felt an obligation to them in return.

The right to fire is also exercised differently by employees than it is by management, with vastly different results, partly because it is far more difficult for a staff member to overturn by appeal or arbitration the collective decision of his or her peers than that of a manager whose motives may be suspect. Also, if an employee can be made more productive, it will be easier for peers to recognize their ability to improve than someone who does not know the employee as well.

They will also be able to encourage the employee through a team effort, rather than pressure a lone employee to improve while she or he is smarting under negative and unsupportive feedback from a manager. Team-based terminations, because they require a consensus, are less frequently the result of personality clashes, communication problems, unclear rules or responsibilities, or perceived hostility, retaliation, and harassment, and are more likely to be a result of a person's actual inability to perform the work.

2. How is Compensation Determined?

Of all the elements in an organizational system, perhaps the greatest difficulty lies in developing a democratic or participative process for determining compensation. From the perspective of a manager, if employees are allowed to decide on their own what pay increases they will receive, they will leave inadequate sums for future investment and pay themselves so much that their costs will make their products or services uncompetitive in the marketplace. Yet our experience has demonstrated that pay cuts and reductions in benefits are more readily agreed to in employee-owned than in non-employee-owned firms.

Several years ago, the Los Angeles Unified School District faced drastic budget cuts by the state of California at the same time that its collective bargaining agreement with the United Teachers of Los Angeles came up for renewal. The bargaining process was extremely difficult and both sides reached impasse several times. Willie Brown, then Speaker of the State Assembly, was brought in to mediate the problem.

Through a process in which full financial information was shared by the district, the union agreed to a 13 percent pay cut. In return, the district agreed to several reforms in the quality of work life for teachers and instructional reform for children. It was clear that the agreement to disclose financial information to the union led to a greater sense of responsibility to create a workable solution. The union did not want bankruptcy any more than the district did.

We have seen a number of alternative solutions work in organizations that are struggling with how to make decisions about compensation and at the same time be consistent with the new paradigm or context. Some of these solutions follow.

- Management mandates or predetermines the total budget and then allows everyone to decide how it should be divided. Schools do this with local, site-based financing.
- The individuals who work for the organization are asked to choose between increased investment with increased future income and lower investment with lower future income and to accept the responsibility for the consequences.
- Management clarifies the cost of competitive products or the realities of the marketplace and educates employees in financial principles so that they can improve their ability to make the right decisions.
- Employees and managers reach consensus on establishing systems that provide monetary rewards for efficiency based on the amounts saved by employee teams, or that reward extra effort, learning, new skills, and other contributions.
- Employees are educated about the results of inefficiency on the finances of the organization and receive rewards for suggestions and cost-cutting initiatives, including a percentage of the profits for suggestions that result in actual financial growth or savings.

- The organization is restructured to make employees equity partners, stockholders, or co-owners, who benefit directly from reduced costs.

These solutions are just a few of the possible measures that can be used to encourage fiscal responsibility consistent with democratic principles and shared decision making.

3. WHO SELECTS THE MANAGERS AND HOW DO THEY MANAGE?

The difference between management and leadership is one that can be seen in many organizations. Management is a role performed by individuals who are designated from above, while leadership is a relationship with those who are below. True leaders are therefore selected, formally or informally, by those they lead. Leadership in one task does not necessarily translate into leadership in any other.

In the self-directed teams with which we have worked, leaders arise spontaneously, by consensus, through an informal mutual selection process based on their ability and willingness to perform a particular task. Their acceptability to other members of the team translates into greater efficiency, productivity, and a higher degree of motivation to follow.

We see leadership expressed by an employee who facilitates a team meeting or who is good at tracking projects or who is willing to be a liaison with other teams or who relates well to customers or who is skilled at mediating disagreements and conflicts between members of the team or who makes sure things don't fall through the cracks. Leadership in a team environment is *situational,* and is shared within the team depending on the job that needs to be done and the skills of each member. Leaders who are selected by their followers have a mandate and can ask for and receive extra effort, which the team does not give freely to a manager who has been imposed from above. Even an elected leader is not a leader in everything, and may simply be the best coordinator or facilitator of the work of others.

While appointed managers are generally more concerned about being accountable to those who are above rather than below them, elected or selected leaders, if they are going to be effective, need to be responsive to those who are below, or rather, alongside them. While this idea may appear unpopular to managers because it would likely result in the replacement of an enormous number of unpopular managers, it would also produce higher morale and greater team spirit, which would result in increased performance and productivity.

Ideally, managerial tasks should be rotated among the ranks so that staff members can better understand their functions and requirements, and vice versa. The ranks of managers can then be kept thin, with as few layers as possible. Management should be a team function, with managers appearing only when necessary to facilitate the work of others, coordinate team efforts, support employees in implementing plans, and ensure that work is done to specification.

The role of the manager is not to control the work process in the name of a higher authority, create bottlenecks, or monopolize positions of power, but rather to facilitate the work of others and make certain it is coordinated in the interest of the organization as a whole. If work tasks are performed conscientiously by employees as a group, there will be little need for managers, but there will always be a need for leaders. For further information on employee leadership, see *Learning To Lead: A Workbook On Becoming A Leader* by Warren Bennis and Joan Goldsmith.

4. WHO GETS PROMOTED, HOW, AND BY WHAT CRITERIA?

In most organizations, promotions are based either on having done a previous job well, which may be completely unrelated to the requirements of the position the employee is seeking, on some guessed-at ability to meet a set of abstract and objective criteria, on purely subjective feelings about the talents or personality of the individual, or on some combination of the above.

In our work with engineering, technology, and financial organizations, we often encounter managers who were excellent at technically performing their work, and are then promoted to nontechnical positions that required "people" skills they never learned. We worked with one manager, Helen, who was a perfect example of what is known as the "Peter Principle." She was an excellent accountant and knew client contracts backwards and forwards, and she was an expert in the company's new computer system. For these reasons, the company placed her in charge of a team, where she was driving her co-workers crazy with her lack of communication and relationship skills.

Helen micromanaged the team's projects and redid all its work, out of fear that it was inadequate. The team saw Helen's work as an effort to prove her own competence, and as a put-down. Helen could not bring herself to give constructive feedback to team members because she was intent on being perceived as "nice," and wanted to please everyone. She could not manage the team or help members allocate their time or follow-up on work assignments and was unable to succeed in her new role. Unfortunately, the manager relied on Helen's technical abilities, failed to judge her ability to manage the work process or lead the team, and didn't equip her with the skills she needed to handle her new position.

Organizations often use promotion as a form of status or as a reward for loyalty or work well done. In many cases, promotion is used to separate people within a hierarchy based on their willingness to obey orders without question or to serve their superiors compliantly or to be "yes men" for people whose egos need stroking in order to bolster their own status or careers. Team selection of team leaders makes the person selected less likely to behave tyrannically and more likely to add to team spirit.

By using job rotation, natural abilities can be observed in practice for each individual, both in terms of objective performance and subjective motivation. Often the reason an employee seeks a promotion is because the new job pays more, grants greater power, offers higher status, or is less physically taxing. Giving team members the ability to select their own leaders and promote their own managers would focus prospective managers on paying greater attention to developing the skills required to manage the group, rather than on their desire for wealth, power, status or comfort.

Ideally, wage rates should be flattened, power should be decentralized, titles should be reduced, and compensation should increase not with status in the hierarchy, but with the employee's skill, level of contribution, knowledge, seniority, difficulty of the task, and willingness to perform even low-status work that benefits the team. If true "market" principles based on job desirability were applied to employment, those performing the least desirable tasks might receive the highest wages.

Motivation for promotion should be based on fulfillment and enjoyment of the tasks required, rather than on increased compensation, laziness, or a desire for power. Internal career counseling, aptitude testing, job rotation, attitude surveys, self-directed teams, and democratic selection are more cost-effective than burnout, laziness, elitism, tyrannical management, and the Peter Principle.

It is possible to motivate people and reward them, not by elevating them over others, but by giving them new choices and challenges; letting them become mentors, trainers, and advisors to those who are still learning; or giving them time to reflect, learn, and increase their skills while rotating managerial tasks throughout the workforce.

For example, Stan was recently selected to be the principal of a public high school in a large urban school district. His first act as principal was to resign. He asked the teachers and staff in the school to select his replacement from among their own ranks, and to rotate this position every three years. He proposed that each new principal, starting with himself, spend his first year performing his duties, his second year sharing those duties and working as a mentor to the next principal, and his third year performing special projects and working as a consultant and advisor to the new principal.

5. WHO ALLOCATES WORK AND ASSIGNS TASKS, AND HOW ARE THEY DONE?

Self-management and task selection by small, self-directed teams has been shown to increase productivity, in part by increasing motivation, but also by limiting the number of unproductive workers and reducing managerial tasks, in a kind of reverse economy of scale. Teamwork allows leadership to operate in a more fluid and dynamic way, rather than in a bureaucratic or static way, and makes managerial awareness the responsibility of everyone in the workforce.

Task-oriented, self-directed teams also help counter the negative effects of isolation due to the separation and division of labor, and improve motivation by increasing task and product identity. These teams can be stable or fast-forming, fixed or flexible, and can take advantage of internal, collaborative competition, as exists, for example, between sports teams in the same geographical area.

Rather than having managers allocate work and assign tasks, many cooperatives, employee-owned enterprises, and traditionally organized companies have found that self-directed teams are able to perform their functions better, with a finer sense of priorities and greater ability to change rapidly in order to meet new demands. Production and service teams can be organized along client, product, problem-solving, or task lines, depending on need. They can be cross-disciplinary and multifunctional or operate within a given skill.

Teams are more capable of knowing what is required at a given moment than a lone manager or central office, which may override a team decision unnecessarily. This does not mean that centralized identification of tasks should be eliminated or performed by employees who do not understand the whole operation. But even these centralized tasks can be handled more efficiently by employees representing different departments than by a single manager or several managers, who often do not intimately know or understand the work process.

Recently, we were asked to help the operations and engineering department of a large corporation reconfigure itself. Dick, the manager, was seen as an obstacle to the delivery of successful customer service because he was a bottleneck for requests. He played favorites by giving assignments to the people he liked, or those he didn't, depending on the task. He often tried to get in and do the work himself, instead of delegating the project to the most knowledgeable person. His manager asked us to work with his department to come up with a solution.

No one wanted to hurt Dick's feelings. He was a nice guy, even if he was an inept manager. Yet everyone was straining under the stress generated by his need to control the allocation of work. During a two-day retreat, we were able to structure a session in which the team gave Dick feedback and put the problem out on the table. Together, they negotiated an alternative role for Dick as a special projects advisor, and the team reached consensus on a new allocation of responsibilities, a new organizational structure, and a new way of setting up job assignments. Everyone breathed a sigh of relief, especially the customers the team served.

6. WHO GETS EDUCATED AND IN WHAT?

Many workers complain that they have not been adequately trained and have to learn their tasks on the job. Managers often know little about how to motivate employees to perform their tasks, how to follow up without micro-managing, how to lead a team effort, how to facilitate a team meeting, or how to teach others to perform their work more skillfully. Few employees are given on-the-job training in effective communication, making formal presentations, collaborative negotiation, taking responsibility for the entire effort, giving honest feedback without creating defensiveness, acknowledging work done well, building better relationships with team members, resolving interpersonal conflicts, or processing work more collaboratively.

Ideally, every organization should consider itself a university in miniature, a "learning organization" as Peter Senge has described it, and provide mandatory and voluntary, free and paid education for its employees based on the needs of the organization and the desires of the workforce.

We can get a better understanding of the power of integrating learning into the work environment from Dr. Edwin Land, who called his Polaroid corporate headquarters "the campus" and saw the company as a place where all employees could enhance their personal and professional skills. Polaroid was one of the first companies in the country to offer employee reimbursement for education and ongoing educational experiences to every level of the organization, including English as a Second Language, Creativity, Total Quality Management, Writing Skills, and Technical Mastery.

Learning is a part of growth and necessary for change, both for individuals and enterprises. The ability to adapt and change is an essential aspect of the modern workplace, and education is a key strategy in transforming the change process from one that is chaotic and adversarial to one that is coherent and cooperative. Long-term employees and those with rich experiences can become teachers and mentors to others. Enormous amounts of skill and knowledge are lost each year to organizations, simply because they have no mechanism for transforming their master-employees into mentors and teachers before they leave the workplace.

As the focus of our work increasingly shifts to arranging and transmitting information, the use of robotics, complex technological systems, computer databases, and so on, a highly trained, continuously learning, and rapidly evolving workforce will become an extremely valuable resource, if not a necessity. In Japan and Germany, companies place considerable emphasis on education and training for employees, with demonstrable results. Employee-focused and -operated education programs will be seen more and more as necessities rather than luxuries.

7. How Is Work Evaluated and Improved?

The old paradigm makes feedback, evaluation, and improvement in the quality of both product and process the exclusive responsibility of management. This arrangement allows employees to become defensive and resistant, managers to play favorites, and no one to be interested in personal or organizational growth. The actual result of feedback and performance evaluation in many old-paradigm organizations is to increase competition and defensiveness, fear of risk taking, avoidance, inability to learn from failure, resentment, wounded feelings, unnecessary conflict, and reduced morale.

Managers who work under the new paradigm and members of self-managing teams that are democratic, participative, and collaborative in their approach, see feedback, evaluation, and improvement as *everyone's* responsibility. In the old paradigm, feedback and evaluation were often used to create punishment, deference, and fear. In the new paradigm, they are used to create improvement, honesty, and risk taking.

In place of the purely hierarchical, downward performance appraisal still used in many organizations, the new evaluation processes work in 360 degrees and include upward, horizontal (peer based), downward, client, and self-analysis as requirements for any meaningful performance evaluation system. Why should employees receive feedback only from managers? Why could not the head of the organization also benefit from periodic performance reviews from those "below"?

The most effective feedback is received from one's direct clients and from one's peers, especially when it is given without threat of punishment and is based on close personal experience. The key to becoming a true learning organization is to provide quick, honest, supportive, and useful evaluations that allow each person to learn, grow, and change with experience.

Tom, a top-level operations manager and a visionary for self-directed teams, provided a model for how "supportive confrontation" in performance evaluation can work. We met with him and his leadership team for a three-day retreat. It was time to turn responsibility for the organization's operations over to the leadership team completely. Tom needed a way to show the team that he was ready to transfer the power to them, so he asked the members to meet without him to decide what their goals were and to give him feedback about what they wanted from him in terms of changed behaviors, more effective support, and his new role as advisor.

At first the team members doubted whether they could be "real" with Tom. We assured them that if self-directed teams were going to work, the honesty would have to begin at the top. They had to take a risk and provide Tom with honest feedback about what they needed from him. Tom's force of personality, vision, and protective behavior toward the team initially hampered its ability to get to the truth. But the team members did it, and while the process was hard for everyone, Tom included, by being direct and honest with him, they became responsible for the success of the organization and became a real team, ready to take on the mantle of leadership themselves.

The most effective way of communicating feedback or conducting a performance evaluation is by beginning with yourself, identifying what was successful in your work and what was not, modeling honesty and risk taking, inviting feedback from everyone else, summarizing their concerns, thanking them for their honesty, and then asking them to evaluate themselves. Risk taking and supportive commentary are best modeled by beginning the process at the top of the organization and having everyone evaluate the performance of the boss. If anyone in the organization is capable of modeling a positive approach to receiving feedback and a genuine willingness to improve, everyone else will be more willing to participate constructively and do the same.

Communication in hierarchies travels downward and sideways much more easily than it travels upward and is blocked by fear the more it tries to become honest. It is therefore critical that judgment be separated from evaluation; that it be peer based rather than hierarchical; that it be done item by item, continuously and immediately, rather than lumped together, saved up, and imposed on employees once every 12 months; that the consequences be implemented nonhierarchically; that feedback be positive and challenging; and that everyone in the organization be open to feedback from all sources.

8. WHO MAKES AND ENFORCES RULES, AND HOW EFFECTIVE ARE THE RULES IN PRACTICE?

Externally imposed rules create obedience, rather than independent thinking, and often generate resistance, which requires coercion, necessitating the creation of an enforcement apparatus. Pretty soon the entire workforce is preoccupied with the process of rule making and discipline, with its distinctions, exceptions, and technicalities. This situation results in the creation of a culture that rewards superficial compliance and uncritical obedience, and forces employees to do what they are told, rather than what they think is right. It also turns managers into police or prison guards, and employees into suspects or prisoners, making it impossible for managers to also be leaders.

Rules that are made and enforced by managers often generate mindless obedience, sabotage, and resistance, but are also far less effective than rules that are generated and voluntarily adopted by employees and enforced by their peers. Given the opportunity, most employees will produce rules for their own behavior that almost exactly parallel those that are developed by managers. When they differ, it is often because a rule was designed to support hierarchy, authority, or managerial power or to bolster the old paradigm of command and control that is unnecessary in a team-based, democratic environment.

For example, most organizations try to discourage gossip and rumors, yet they behave in ways that actually encourage these behaviors. Any effort to control information from the top automatically produces a response by those at the bottom who fill in the gaps with gossip, rumors, and guesswork as a substitute for facts they were not given. Gossip and rumor are a kind of negative glue in many organizations; they are used to create a sense of security, intimacy, community, and power, often at the expense of others. They help people read between the lines and figure out what is likely to happen to them, but they also encourage misinformation, character assassination, cliques, factions, and secrets, as well as block open, honest, and authentic communication.

We worked recently with the faculty, administration, and staff of a community college in a strategic planning process. The college was rife with tension, factions, and cliques who used gossip and rumors as a way of compensating for their feelings of being left out of the decision-making process, and as a way of communicating their resentment by fanning the flames of dissension. We spent hours discussing these negative personal and organizational patterns, and all participants agreed they were behaving like members of a dysfunctional family.

One small group that was working on strategies for improved communications came up with a suggestion that everyone go on a "gossip diet." Their announcement was followed by spontaneous applause. The new rules stated that if anyone started to gossip, recipients were to respond by saying they were on a gossip diet and would not participate unless the gossipmonger had communicated his or her complaint, concern, or question to the person who was involved, or to someone who could do something about the problem. This gossip diet could never have been imposed by the president or dictated by the faculty council. It could only have been created through consensus by the community acting as a whole.

If all employees understand that they have a vested interest in improving the methods of work and increasing productivity and client satisfaction, they will automatically cooperate in creating the rules, both formal and informal, that advance their common interests. This atmosphere will create feelings of shared ownership and shared management of the organization. It is only when employees believe that their fundamental interests differ, and that a win for one will necessarily result in a loss for the others, that adversarial competition results.

Disputes often occur, for example, in top-down organizations over how resources should be allocated, how money should be spent, how much people should be paid in salaries, or where each person should be in the hierarchy. These disputes are a wasteful diversion from the business of the organization and unnecessarily divide employees into hostile camps. As a result of these adversarial contests, rules are promulgated to keep the peace, coercion becomes necessary to enforce the rules, and the organization can't win no matter what it decides.

Moreover, while rules are by nature objective, enforcement is often subjective, and a double standard often arises in organizations based on personal favoritism, perceived power, race and gender identification, or social status. If rules are to be fair, enforcement should also be democratized. There is no reason why an entire workforce cannot decide what the rules should be, how they should be enforced, or what the consequences will be for breaking them. All employees can then feel truly responsible for carrying out the rules. The team process is thus both an alternative to top-down rule making and a method for enforcing compliance once consensus has been reached.

A year ago, we were asked to mediate a dispute in which an employee for a small firm had been fired by his supervisor for taking time away from work to run a personal errand. When we asked the supervisor whether he would accept the employee back, the supervisor answered that he would because he was soft hearted, but that the other employees probably would not. We asked the employee about it, and he said he would accept the verdict of his co-workers if his boss agreed to do likewise. The boss agreed, and the issue was presented to the worker's peers for a decision. They discussed the issues for an hour and decided to terminate him, not because of the minor incident for which he had been caught, but because they knew he had been cheating and stealing from the company for a long time. The employee accepted the decision without a challenge.

9. WHO DEALS WITH CONFLICTS AND HOW ARE THEY RESOLVED?

In most workplaces, managers spend enormous amounts of time trying to cover up, manage, resolve, or deal with the consequences of conflicts in the workplace. The total time that is lost to conflict includes wasted time in pointless arguments and petty jealousies, shame and anger taken out in sick time and absenteeism, and time spent simply handling the stress, fear, worry, and preoccupation that goes along with being in the middle of a conflict. There are also organizational costs to conflict, including the spread of negativity, the effects of poor morale, the time wasted on gossip and rumors, the money spent on attorneys and lawsuits, and the time spent by managers figuring out how to solve the conflict. If all these amounts are added up, the true cost of conflict is overwhelming, particularly when we realize that nearly all workplace conflicts are preventable, manageable, and resolvable at a fraction of the time and cost we spend being stuck in them.

Workers in Chinese organizations, for example, elect mediators from among their peers to resolve conflicts in every work unit and team. In the United States, conflicts between employees, teams, and managers are also successfully mediated, occasionally by peers who are elected by the group but more often by neutral outside mediators. Professional mediators often use consensus to help resolve organizational and intergroup conflicts before they become serious.

During the past 14 years, we have often been retained to mediate interpersonal and organizational disputes ranging from sexual harassment complaints and wrongful termination to conflicts among and between managers, teams, departments and co-workers. Mediation is successful largely because it is a voluntary, consensus-based process that is highly democratic and extraordinarily effective, particularly when combined with activities designed to prevent the future occurrence of conflict. It therefore fits in perfectly with the new paradigm.

A new field of "conflict resolution systems design" proposes using a conflict audit to determine the sources of conflict; providing extensive training in communication, negotiation, and problem solving; looking for ways of affecting the sources of chronic conflict; identifying the early warning signs of resolvable conflict; creating safety nets; designing techniques for prevention, management, and early resolution; providing loop-backs to negotiation; and using low-cost procedures such as arbitration as a backup. These ideas are developed in greater detail in Section 7.

Consensus-based conflict-resolution processes increase organizational efficiency by improving morale, providing an outlet for emotional venting, reducing resistance, encouraging listening, and making it acceptable to talk openly and honestly about what everyone is gossiping about in secret. They encourage compassion, empathy, forgiveness, growth, personal change, and ethical behavior and also help order the chaos generated by dysfunctional systems, poor communication, and rapid organizational change.

We were called in several years ago to mediate a dispute in a community organization in which the managers were creating chaos and poor morale among the secretaries and others in the office by yelling and engaging in aggressive, angry behavior. We worked with both groups to clarify their roles, responsibilities, and expectations and negotiated agreements about what would happen if their behaviors did not change. They ended up reaching a satisfactory agreement and improving their relationships with each other, and the secretaries and managers decided to each select a representative to be trained in mediation to jointly resolve future disputes. For further information on conflict resolution, see *Mediation, Revenge and the Magic of Forgiveness* by Kenneth Cloke.

10. HOW ARE PROFITS AND LOSSES DIVIDED?

Our experiences with self-directed employee teams have clearly shown that employees can competently participate in making important organizational decisions, consistently work to improve their effectiveness, and take responsibility for the success of the group as a whole. Based on that experience, it is only a question of time before employee involvement is extended to making decisions regarding the allocation of profits and losses, resources, equipment, buildings, and other issues traditionally decided by owners or top-level managers. We see no reason why employees cannot participate responsibly in deciding how to allocate the surpluses and deficits of organizations to which they are committed.

Employee-owned organizations and worker cooperatives appear to make these decisions quite well. One reason for a great deal of poor decision making regarding the workplace is the demand for short-term profits by shareholders whose only stake in the organization is the money they earn from it. The more long-term concerns for employee morale, or even for stable growth and customer service, often tend to take second place in shareholder decision making.

A large for-profit company, which engaged us recently, tried to reengineer its work processes and found senior managers resisting the changes. In an environment that offered executives great latitude to run their own departments, the shift to a more integrated, cross-functional model was perceived as reducing their power. The executives who sponsored the reengineered process were seeking ways to change the behavior of their managers without dictating outcomes that would only be sabotaged.

The executives decided to put their own interests on the line for the new organization and agreed that 50 percent of their bonuses would be based on the success of the organization as a whole in migrating to the new plan. They then took this compensation model to the senior managers and asked them what it would take to have them do the same. What surfaced in the discussion was the fear and uncertainty that lay just beneath the resistance. Questions about executive support, concerns about their own skill levels, and unknowns about motivating and trusting their employees came to the fore. At the end of the meeting, the senior managers decided to change their own compensation package as well and base half of their bonuses on successful implementation of the new organization.

In other organizations we have worked with that are moving to self-directed teams, it quickly becomes clear to both managers and employees that the change to employee responsibility and self-direction cannot take place unless the compensation system is redesigned to reward the extra effort that is required. Organizations are beginning to use many innovative ideas to share profits with employees, ranging from pay-for-learning and pay-for-skills to bonuses, stock options, gain sharing, cooperatives, and outright employee ownership. If personal ownership and financial gain are strong motivators in our own lives, why not extend them to everyone in the workplace and create an ongoing interest in the success of the organization?

Employees have a strong ongoing interest in sustainable growth and may actually be better at making decisions regarding long-term growth and investment than are individual shareholders who do not always see the long-term possibilities because they are focused on quarterly dividends. Employees are also more likely to make better informed decisions because their own futures and those of their families depend on their choices. The same points can be made for nonprofit organizations regarding budgeting, resource allocation, and financial decisions.

We believe the old paradigm, where the owner or shareholders had the sole power to advance money to the organization and set the compensation for its employees, is giving way to a new paradigm, which recognizes the higher responsibility of those who work in the organization and ultimately produce its success.

Conclusion

As you consider these ideas and the new paradigms they represent, we would like you to look deeply at the consequences that are involved in changing even one element in your organizational system. As we pointed out at the beginning of this chapter, these elements are all part of an integrated package that is bound up inextricably with the dominant paradigm. If you rethink one aspect of your organization, the entire paradigm will necessarily come into play. Since every organization is an integrated system, success at changing one element forces others to shift.

We suggest that humanized workplaces and democratically organized self-directed teams fundamentally alter the way we think about the whole of our work environment and require us to reexamine every aspect of the way we work, including the way we change. We begin the next chapter with a practical examination of the change process and encourage you to redesign not only the way you work, but also the way you implement these changes, so that you can better meet your own needs, along with those of your co-workers, colleagues, clients, and customers.

Our purpose has been to begin the rethinking process, not to end it. Rethinking the way we work is not something that should be done once and then forgotten, but often and continuously, and for every aspect of our work environment. Moreover, we want to encourage you not to accept what we have said here at face value, but to explore on your own, using this book as a guide to inquiry, rather than as a set of answers that are fixed in stone.

The regular questioning of fundamental assumptions is a prerequisite for learning, both for individuals and organizations that are trying to be successful in a changing environment. This task is not easy, but it is one you can master if you move a step at a time and approach it strategically. If you engage in this process with others in your workplace, you will be far more successful than if you try it alone. Remember, you have only your paradigms to lose!

SIX

Embracing Change

It must be considered that there is nothing more difficult, nor more doubtful of success, nor more dangerous to handle than to initiate a new order of things. For the reformer has enemies in all those who profit by the old order, and only lukewarm defenders in all those who would profit by the new order, this lukewarmness arising . . . partly from the incredulity of mankind, who do not truly believe in anything new until they have had actual experience of it.

NICCOLO MACHIAVELLI, 1513

Embracing Change in Our Work Lives

Larry, a vice president of a large finance organization, decided to shift his department to self-directed teams. Midway through the process, he told us he wanted to turn the task of managing these teams over to a group of his direct reports. After the group struggled to define its role as a leadership team, the members decided to let Larry know what they needed and expected of him. They quickly came to the conclusion that for the group to succeed in providing leadership, Larry had to change his role in the organization, and the only ones who would tell Larry what he needed to change were the people who reported to him.

Their requests included some straightforward actions such as being a liaison to upper management on their behalf; serving as a buffer with other departments; helping them create a vision to guide their future direction; and providing information about the big picture of mergers, acquisitions, and trends in the industry. But they also wanted Larry to change his behavior, which was difficult because it meant he had to change his entire management style, or what seemed to him like his personality.

Douglas McGregor in *The Professional Manager* described Larry's challenge this way:

The important point about the difference between changing tactics and changing style is that the former is usually easy, while the latter is complex and difficult. It is difficult because it is potentially threatening—or at least it is perceived as threatening to the manager's basic adjustment, to his role as he conceives it. Logical argument, persuasion, managerial policy decisions, and even direct pressure are seldom effective in bringing about significant alterations in style.

The members of the leadership team wanted Larry to do more coaching and mentoring; to acknowledge them and their teams more frequently; to be more open to feedback without becoming defensive or seeking retribution; to give them room to take greater risks without fearing his disapproval; and to be more sensitive in his choice of words and tone of voice when giving them feedback.

McGregor was right; it took a major commitment on Larry's part to change his style. It also required the team's willingness to risk giving him honest and immediate feedback whenever he slipped back into his old behaviors, as well as the team's ability to coach Larry as he experimented with new ways of working and responding to criticism that would help him become more effective in a team environment.

The challenge for you, as we focus in this chapter on implementing change, is to look at whether you need to shift *your* style, and at the paradigms that have shaped your behaviors, even when these contexts and behaviors have produced a certain level of success. The heart of the question we are posing here is: Are you willing, as Larry was, to try something new when the old ways of working are not yet clearly and completely outmoded? Can you let go of what you have become accustomed to and successful at and open yourself to the insecurity that is a necessary part of change?

In many ways, it is easier for us to change when we are in the midst of a crisis. When we become comfortable with the way things are, we stop growing and learning. If we are afraid of change, we become unable to see that the old, comfortable paradigm is no longer taking us where we need or want to go. So the challenge is to make the difficult changes, the ones that require a new style, a new world view, new skills, and new ways of managing, so that we develop into leaders who can make these changes a reality.

It will also be useful to look closely at the change process itself and to start developing a new model for *how* we bring about change. If we try to shift to a new paradigm using behaviors and change processes developed under the old one, we will end up re-creating what we most need to change. Einstein wrote: "Our problems cannot be solved by the same level of thinking that created them."

We have gradually developed a working model of change over many years by observing ourselves and others throughout the change process, and by evaluating the behaviors and attitudes, that contributed to the change effort. The model we discuss and explore in the pages that follow is based on these behaviors and attitudes which we believe will help you to implement successful changes in your organization and workplace. We believe these successful behaviors and attitudes are:

- Being willing to change.
- Understanding our reactions to change.
- Being an empowering leader.
- Facing difficult issues and conflicts.
- Organizing the change process.
- Planning strategically.
- Focusing on producing results.
- Humanizing the change process.
- Becoming effective change agents.

These behaviors are not stages, but processes that need to be repeated throughout the change process. We know that the distinctions between many of these behaviors are in some respects artificial, and that it is possible to engage in all these behaviors and have the change fail. We have delineated them so that you can focus on each one, master it, and discover for yourself where you want to put the emphasis for your own growth. We know it is not easy to embrace change and be successful at it. We know it feels more comfortable to stay in our ruts and rationalize or justify the way we have behaved in the past. Edith Wharton wrote powerfully of this attraction we have for our ruts in *A Backward Glance*:

> Years ago I said to myself: "There's no such thing as old age; there is only sorrow." I have learned with the passing of time that this, though true, is not the whole truth. The other producer of old age is habit: the deathly process of doing the same thing in the same way at the same hour day after day, first from carelessness, then from inclination, at last from cowardice or inertia. Luckily the inconsequent life is not the only alternative; for caprice is as ruinous as routine. Habit is necessary; it is *the* habit of having habits, of turning a trail into a rut, that must be incessantly fought against if one is to remain alive. *[Emphasis added.]*

The danger for most organizations is that the habit of having habits keeps us from seeing how stuck we have become. In the sections that follow, we ask you to examine your habit of having habits and consider becoming more willing to embrace change. We suggest you try these ideas on as though they were a new hat, or a pair of shoes, to see whether they fit. Our experience leads us to believe they will help you more fully understand, participate in, and be successful throughout the change process.

Being Willing to Change

We have illustrated the power of commitment in bringing about change through the story of Larry's transformation. While most of us would describe ourselves as being open to change, very few of us have been successful at changing either our deepest habits or those of other people. We really change only when we genuinely want to, not because someone else tries to force change upon us. None of us wants to be changed by anyone other than ourselves.

We can learn from the experience of Alcoholics Anonymous that even people who are addicted and most resistant to change are nonetheless able to transform themselves and alter their behavior. But we also learn that it is not possible to change an addict until she or he wants to change. In some ways, we and the people we work with are also addicts, holding on to the false security of our old addictive contexts and paradigms, rather than face the insecurity of change. And like addicts, we deny that we are addicted, but find we cannot give up our old habits, and we continue behaving in the old way.

Yet if hundreds of thousands of alcoholics and drug addicts can face their addictions honestly and transform their lives, it is not hopeless for us to think we can change our organizations, our work lives, and the way we work. In our experience, it is not only possible, but necessary and rewarding to do so, but only when we choose to change—not just in the abstract or in theory, but in reality.

Several years ago, we facilitated a consensus decision-making process for a large urban high school that received a grant of nearly $1,000,000 to restructure itself. The grant had been the result of a long and difficult planning process that had involved the entire faculty and staff. But when the money actually arrived and it was time for implementation, members of the faculty and staff were suddenly confronted with the need to actually change the way they organized their day, how they taught their students, what materials they used, and how they worked together. As one faculty member put it, "I thought it was the school and everyone else who had to change. I never thought it meant I had to."

Everything begins with our commitment to make the change happen. Only later are we able to convince others, on the basis of our commitment, to participate with us and provide the support we need to make the change succeed. All the changes we have experienced in our lives, and in the history of the world, began with the commitment of a single person. And there is magic in that commitment. As W. H. Murray wrote in *The Scottish Himalayan Expedition*:

> *Until one is committed there is hesitancy, the chance to draw back, always ineffectiveness. Concerning all acts of initiative (and creation), there is one elementary truth, the ignorance of which kills countless ideas and splendid plans: that the moment one definitely commits oneself, then Providence moves too. All sorts of things occur to help one that would never otherwise have occurred. A whole stream of events issues from the decision, raising in one's favour all manner of unforeseen incidents and meetings and material assistance, which no man could have dreamt would have come his way. I have learned a great respect for one of*

Goethe's couplets: 'Whatever you can do, or dream you can, begin it. Boldness has genius, power, and magic in it.'

Being willing to change means examining everything, even your own job, to see what it contributes to the organization. We recently facilitated the redesign of a large governmental division that administered 13 universities. The purpose of the project was to support the leader of those universities in radically transforming their institutions from top to bottom. Before we took the job, we asked the administrative organization whether it was willing to question everything, including the existence of its own organization. When the answer was yes, we knew we could take · on the assignment. Are you willing to take the same risks with your organization? What roles, responsibilities, structures, or systems are you unwilling to put on the table?

Understanding Our Reactions to Change

Once we commit ourselves to bringing about a necessary change, our work is not over. We need to center ourselves, to objectively assess our own skills and abilities, and to understand how many of our attitudes, skills, and reactions to change have deep roots in our early life histories.

When we are in the midst of the change process, it is often difficult to see where we are heading, or even know what we are feeling. One of our clients put it this way:

Change is so difficult and sometimes as insiders we can't see the forest for the trees. We've needed tools to help get outside the forest and see the shape and form of it from a higher level.

Part of the difficulty is that we come to the change process with a number of prior experiences that influence how we see, imagine, and participate in it. The following exercise provides an opportunity for you to get outside the change process and reflect on your history, your patterns, and the ways you tend to participate in the changes that have happened in your life.

Understanding Our Reactions to Change: An Exercise

To begin with, please reflect for a moment on how the changes that have taken place in your life may have affected your attitude toward change itself. When we refer to life changes, we mean large-scale shifts in how you see yourself, your life, your past, and your future. These experiences may include marriage or divorce; a sudden realization about the role your parents played in your life; having children; a new awareness of your life priorities; a death or other loss; a geographical move; a change in social class; an illness that altered your mobility or vitality; or the loss of a cherished belief or ideology. When changes such as these take place as, for example, following a death, our whole world shifts and life becomes suddenly very different, altering us so profoundly that we can never return to our former selves.

You first learned about change in your family. How did your parents respond to change? Did they seek stability or live on the edge, courting change? Did you learn in adolescence to "go with the flow" or to be different, to take risks or look for certainties in your life? Did you select a field or career that promised constancy, or have you searched for new adventures?

Take a look at yourself, and spend a moment in the exercise below becoming more aware of what you do, feel, and think when you encounter a significant change in your life. To complete this exercise, you will need to sit in a quiet place, either by yourself or with others who are also ready for a period of reflection.

1. Begin by selecting one of the major changes from your past, such as one of those mentioned above. You may be going through one of these changes right now. If so, please choose that one. Briefly describe the change below.

   _____

   _____

   _____

2. Try to remember how you felt before the change began. What was happening in your life? How were you behaving? Who was with you? What did you think and feel about yourself?

   _____

   _____

   _____

3. Now, try to remember the change itself. How did it happen? How was it initiated? What was your initial reaction to it? Did your reactions change over time? How did the change affect your view of yourself and your life?

    _____

    _____

    _____

4. How has the change affected your view of yourself today? Did a paradigm change for you? If so, how would you characterize that change?

    _____

    _____

    _____

5. What enabled you to embrace the new paradigm and integrate it into your life? If you haven't changed your paradigm but would like to, what it would take for you to do so?

    _____

    _____

    _____

As your reflect on your past experiences with change and your reactions to them, see if you can discover a pattern in how you have dealt with change. Is there anything you can learn from this example about how you are responding to changes that are taking place at work now? What would you like to take from your past experience and apply to the present? What would you like to do differently?

By heightening your awareness of the responses you have had to change, you can improve your ability to participate in transforming the contexts and paradigms you face at work. The more aware you are of these patterns, the easier it will be to make the shift. You may say to yourself: I see now. I'm skeptical of the transformations taking place at work because of the impact of a previous change in my personal life. I need to measure these new ideas at the workplace against my belief system and make sure I am not just resisting the change because of an earlier similar experience.

Every person chooses how to respond to a proposed change based not only on their agreement or disagreement with what is being proposed, but based on their life histories, their needs, their personal styles, and their desires for the future. If we are cynical or apathetic or angry about life, we will tend to bring these same emotions to the change process. The point is not to suppress these emotions, histories, needs, or desires, but to be aware of them, and to be able to act freely on the basis of choice, without responding because of some invisible compulsion.

Being an Empowering Leader

All change requires leadership, not in the sense of a single person who "leads the way" to the exclusion of all others, but in terms of people who empower others to make a difference. The leaders in the civil rights movement were not just courageous individuals like Rosa Parks or Martin Luther King Jr., but thousands of equally courageous people who walked to work as part of the boycott that ended segregated bus transportation in Montgomery, Alabama. Leadership is not something "they" do. It is also up to each of us to become leaders in our own lives.

One way of successfully bringing about the changes we have discussed is to realize that we are all capable of being leaders, and that teams encourage leadership not just among managers, but among all ranks of employees. Everyone needs to develop the "people skills" that are essential to leadership and to a humanized workplace. Two employees we worked with in a changing information systems organization described the needs of their organization as follows:

If we are really going to change we need basic skills, analysis, the technical skills, but also leadership skills for working closely with the client community which also needs, by the way, to change—because they'll be heavily impacted as well. In information systems, we're great at creating changes but we don't know how to manage changes. Change management will be a critical skill—and so will good communications.

People skills will be required. Some groups have it, some don't; some have extensive TQM or Deming, and others have nothing. We'll change the technology and bring it into a new century but then folks will need leadership, project management skills, people skills, and we don't have the experience to do this.

One of the hardest lessons leaders have to learn is that we cannot control the change process, either for ourselves or for others. People who are going through a significant change need time and space to understand their own reactions and manage them. Many managers make the mistake of trying to over-control their employees, missing the contributions their staff members can make based on their different paces, skills, and perspectives. The following comments made by middle managers about a chief information officer with whom we worked point dramatically to this problem:

> I think David does not want to fall into old modes. He wants to push the organization very hard to go forward. He wants to push it fast, but at the same time he feels the need to have control over the direction. That's OK, but he has to let people run the organization. There's reasons for him to do what he's doing, but somehow he's got to let people do their jobs. You need alignment—you've got to make sure everyone's on the same page and if you are going to get it from the middle manager up, I think you have to get buy-in, not control for it.

> David needs to trust his management to handle the change. He hired us because we have skills and experience. He needs to let us do what he hired us to do. Sometimes I can't make decisions because he can't let go. He thinks he can control everything but he can't. He should be focusing on policy and strategy and representing us with senior management and not micro-managing our every move through the change.

Rather than controlling and micromanaging the work, David's leadership was needed to give direction and support to each person in finding his or her own style and way of responding to the change. When "command and control" is the approach from the top, employees distrust their own ability to handle the glitches that inevitability occur during the change process. If they distrust themselves, they will distrust their leaders and resist following them into the new paradigm. One of our clients in the early stages of a major change process observed:

> People do not yet trust the leaders. The leaders need to change their behaviors, they must walk the talk consistently. They have not given us the authority to make the day-to-day decisions. When people come to me for little decisions I tell them to just go ahead and do it. But we don't get the guidance and clear definition on what we will continue and not continue to do. Sometimes the leadership group doesn't give clear leadership on the overall picture. We should teach managers and project leaders that part of their job is to support the people who are working for them. Teach them how to give credit and not take it for themselves. It is critical to build confidence and trust.

Facing Difficult Issues and Conflicts

In addition to committing ourselves to change, understanding our personal reactions to it, and seeing ourselves as empowering leaders, another element in successfully organizing a change process is for the advocates of the change to honestly face and fully understand its difficulties and consequences. We coached the management team of a service department in a Fortune 100 manufacturing company through a change process and heard the following comment:

People do not have an appreciation for the complex issues they will run into when they roll out solutions and a new infrastructure to the clients. We have a complex organization. There are union plants, non-union plants, team players, and lone rangers out there. Work processes differ from plant to plant. The day to day work lives of our clients will change and no one understands the significance of that, either the challenge or the fun. We have to understand the nature, quality and quantity of the changes we are proposing.

To bring about a significant change in the workplace, we first need to understand the nature of the problem that needs to be solved. If, for example, we are working in an organization that has decided to create self-directed teams, we first need to know what problems these self-directed teams are supposed to solve. Are we going to teams because we are trying to produce more revenue, provide better client service, make everyone feel better, deal with gaps created by downsizing, or gain greater access to employee talent and contribution?

Once we know what the problem is, we can begin to articulate a vision of how the new participatory environment will look, feel, and behave, instead of immediately plunging into designating teams and putting them to work. We can use the envisioning process to help employees understand that there is an alternative to the way they have been working that promises to be better than what they have now, and create an opportunity for dialogue over what is most important to them, so they can start with a positive step, rather than a negative one.

After creating a vision of where the people in the organization want to go, we can start to identify all the things that stand in the way of its realization, including the problems, dysfunctions, criticisms, unresolved conflicts, and barriers to success that exist in every workplace. In the context of a vision, problems can be seen as *challenges* or hurdles rather than obstacles, as harbingers of a context or paradigm shift that can be discerned through the gaps, anomalies, and disjunctures in the way things work.

Talking openly and honestly about our problems can be liberating. We worked recently with the faculty, staff, and parents of a 4,000-pupil urban high school. We asked mixed teams to list all the problems that prevented them from providing an excellent education for all their children. This was the moment the teachers and staff had been waiting for, a chance to air all their personal grievances! We asked them to make sure the parents also had an opportunity to discuss the problems they faced, and not to horde their problems and keep them to themselves, only to discount the process later because we didn't address their secret needs.

After about 20 minutes, we began to hear raucous laughter, loud talk, and saw signs of great teamwork and camaraderie. The teams reported experiencing tremendous relief and even enjoyed talking about their problems. Individuals found that they were not alone, and that others shared their points of view. After spilling out a myriad of problems, we asked them to pick the most powerful ones, the underlying ones, those that were at the source of their difficulties, and those that would give the school the greatest leverage for change. We then asked them to take these problems on and come up with creative ideas for solutions. Everyone was asked to join a "Solution Team," to get on board and make the change happen. Everyone in the school joined in, and most of the problems that had been identified had already disappeared.

The reason the entire school community was willing to become actively involved in making these changes happen was that people had talked about the problems openly and constructively, and in the process, had actually experienced their teams as places where the problems they described *did not exist.* When everyone was asked to join a small team to describe their problems, inclusion, open communication, honesty, and trust ceased to be barriers.

Identifying Organizational Problems:
An Exercise

We would like you to participate in a similar exercise now, and if possible, to do so in a group or team that represents every constituency in your work organization. You can rate the problems we have listed below, or make your own list of the ones you see in your organization, and then compare them with our list. The rating system works by ranking each item from 1 to 5 based on the degree to which it affects your organization, with 1=no effect and 5=great effect. We have provided space to add additional problems.

1. Overlapping job functions. —
2. Gaps in responsibility. —
3. Work overload and stress. —
4. Under utilization of talent. —
5. Unclear roles and responsibilities. —
6. Functional opposition in the same organization or unit. —
7. Employee isolation. —
8. Unnecessary needs to request permission to act. —
9. Meeting proliferation and uselessness. —
10. Excessive rules and policies. —
11. Confusion over decision-making authority. —
12. Lack of coordination or consensus regarding direction. —
13. Inflexibility. —
14. Inappropriate technology. —
15. Inability to change. —
16. Lack of desire or opportunity to listen. —
17. Environmental insensitivity. —
18. Lack of opportunity for growth or learning. —
19. Lack of vision. —
20. Lack of strategic thinking. —
21. Hierarchical, one-way communication. —
22. Competition for resources. —
23. Exploitative wages. —
24. Lack of consumer protection. —
25. Inadequate safety precautions. —
26. Racial, ethnic, gender, cultural, age, or handicap discrimination. —

27. Silencing of criticism and inability
   to learn from failure.   —
28. Turf battles.   —
29. Defensive as opposed to
   proactive behavior.   —
30. Personal attack and adversarial
   approach to conflict.   —
   [Add your own problems here.]

———————————————————————

———————————————————————

If you are working with others in your organization, discuss the ratings each of you gave to the problems listed above. Talk about the specifics of these dysfunctional characteristics. Come up with stories, examples, and experiences. Flesh out the issues so everyone understands what the problems are. Get them all out so you can face the barriers head-on. If discrepancies exist, share your perceptions so that everyone is able to develop a deeper understanding of how these problems play themselves out. This exercise may give you a better view of the cracks in your organizational system. It will also normalize and make it acceptable for you to have an open conversation about your problems, allow new ideas and justifications to emerge for shifting the context or paradigm, and encourage improvement in your organization.

Organizing the Change Process

If we think of change as a *holistic* process that combines what we want to change with how we are going to change it, we will be much more successful in bringing it about. Our process and our content need to be consistent with each other, and our actions and values need to be congruent.

Learning about how to be effective in bringing about change is a lifelong process. We are always searching for useful information from people who are steeped in the change process, including community activists, internal and external corporate consultants, school change coaches, innovative employees, nonprofit organizers, and organizational leaders who have a vision. All of these players have useful experiences we can learn from in understanding how people respond to change.

We would like to share with you some of the ideas we have gathered from our own experiences and from other change agents who have sought to shift their communities, organizations, and societies. If you have tried to humanize your workplace or change your organization or community, you probably have a list of your own.

The following set of generic change management suggestions might apply equally to organizing impoverished communities, mobilizing county employees, and shifting the direction of nonprofit organizations, urban schools or Fortune 500 companies. These suggestions concern the nature of the change process and how it can be influenced by conscious, interconnected human activity.

As you reflect on your own experiences and those of your colleagues, notice the principles that you have learned and add them at the end of the list; then share them with your co-workers. Some of the ideas we think you might be able to use to get started, to encourage the change process, to be more strategic, and to generate less resistance, include the following:

1. **Analyze the structural divisions that fragment your organization and devise ways of bringing together people who have been separated by narrow or isolating self-interests.** For example, we often ask employees and managers to create a "true" chart of how their organization actually operates, including internal divisions between "stovepipe" departments, salary grades, job titles, races, cultures, genders, social classes, geographical locations, and specializations that create divergent cultures and cliques within the organization. Then we analyze how these barriers block internal communication and teamwork across the organization. We then create cross-functional, cross-level, cross-cultural and cross-geographical work teams to tackle particular problems.

2. **Make the human dimensions of the change understandable and personal.** For example, we often try to create personal empathy with everyone in the change process, sometimes by asking those involved to tell stories of "the good old days" or show photographs from the past or bring artifacts from their culture to share. Then everyone can empathize with everyone else and begin to accept feelings of loss or isolation. Or we may ask people early in the process to tell personal "success stories" or relate their "best

practices" to one another. All these techniques personalize the change process and help create participation, consensus, and buy-in.

3. **Articulate a justification for the changes you are advocating by referring to shared values or history or the self-interests of those you are trying to help change.** Sometimes we ask people on opposite sides of an argument, for example, union and management negotiating teams or conflicting parties in a mediation, to talk about their shared history or the values or goals they have in common. If they are in conflict, we may ask people on each side to summarize the other side's interests, to explain how they would have reacted if they had been on the other side, to role play the part of the opposition, or to create a statement that reflects their values or position, in other words, "to walk a mile in the other person's shoes."

4. **Speak openly and honestly about unacceptable behavior while demonstrating unconditional acceptance for the people who are engaging in it.** We often cite our friend Bill Ury's distinction (developed with Roger Fisher in *Getting to Yes*), of the need to separate the person from the problem, to be simultaneously hard on the problem and soft on the people. People's behaviors may cause problems, but the behaviors should not be confused with the people. We need to treat people as potential allies so they will not become enemies, and people need to understand that they can change their actions without feeling judged or excluded from the process.

5. **Look for ways of changing not only the content, but also the methods and processes that reinforce and recreate it.** For example, if an executive or manager decides to send a message to staff that she is receptive to feedback or that "my door is always open," yet fails to show up for meetings on time or responds defensively to criticism or takes phone calls during problem solving sessions, the process will completely invalidate the message she said she wanted to send. Staff members will see the content of the manager's stated intention as a contradiction to the method or process used to achieve it. If we want to change the content of our relationships with others, we also need to change the processes we use to define it.

6. **Actively support both diversity and unity, independence and collective action, individuality and community, difference of opinion and consensus.** We often begin trainings on prejudice reduction and bias awareness by asking everyone in the room to indicate how they are different from one another, for example, by asking them to tell the group four things they are proud of about their culture, race, gender, or background. Because we spend a great deal of time during the workshop exploring and validating differences, the group is also able to see more clearly what they have in common, and paradoxically ends up with stronger feelings of unity, community, and togetherness.

7. **Accept everyone, wherever they happen to be at the time, and look for ways of encouraging them to move forward.** Do not judge people for where they began or where they have moved to, but help them understand their ability to move farther and faster. For example, in team feedback sessions, we may ask each person to indicate their goals for their own personal behavior. Each person then indicates where he or she feels a need to improve, and others are able to add their perceptions and support. The team process does not work if we use the same yardstick for everyone. Each person's starting place is real and valid. The only appropriate questions are, Do you want to move to a different place? Where and when will you begin? How can I support you?

8. **Create an internal sense of community, of belonging and acceptance. Situate the change in a social environment that is open and hospitable.** A dean we know turned one of the most conservative and traditional universities in the country upside down by holding an informal "down-time open house" every Friday in his offices. Anyone and everyone had access to Paul weekly and was welcome to come and hang out with him and his staff. He created a sense of belonging and openness while driving major changes around him, in large part because he created a broad sense of belonging and acceptance. The deeper the change, the greater the need for support.

9. **Establish links with the larger community, with customers or clients, including formal and informal leaders, community**

organizations, social groups, and the locations where people gather. A headstart program we worked with wanted to involve parents to a greater extent in order to change their experience of education for their children and demonstrate principles of lifelong learning. The staff asked the mothers what the school could provide that would support them in participating more actively in the school. The mothers said they really wanted sewing machines so they could come to school, make clothes for their children, and have a place where they could help their families while their children learned alongside them.

10. **Celebrate not only the visionaries of the change process, but also the implementers, and do not diminish the role of one simply because it is not the other.** Some of us like to blaze trails or are good at startups and high-risk ventures. Others want to build something lasting, or have a talent for day-to-day implementation. Neither of these tasks is more important or valuable than the other. We need to have both, or we end up creating visions that are never implemented and implementing ideas that are not worthwhile.

11. **Beware of conceit and "powerism," of the narcotic of leadership, of attitudes of self-righteousness and entitlement, and of the corruption of task-oriented sacrifice in the name of expediency and results.** Two of the most difficult attitudes we have encountered in the change process are those that worship power and see people as disposable, and those at the other end that celebrate martyrdom. People who fall under the sway of power or get seduced by the sound of their own voices stop listening altogether. People who become martyrs are working so hard and doing so much that they don't take time to involve or empower others. Both types of behavior are covers for people who are afraid they will lose their sense of identity and self-worth if they give up their special roles, and both are forms of undermining or disempowering others.

12. **Exercise leadership by taking direction from those who follow.** A good leader is one who catches up quickly with his or her "followers" once they have begun to move. A new manager took over a division in a manufacturing unit that was

organized in self-managing teams. His first act was to schedule a two-hour meeting with each team to engage in open conversation about how he might support them in achieving their goals. He asked them about their priorities before sharing his own, and listened to their needs for clarity of vision and direction, for additional resources, and for team training. Six months later, he gave them a scorecard to complete on how well he had performed and delivered. His ratings were higher than those of any previous manager because he had listened and taken direction from below.

13. **Direct the change process to have an impact on the organizational system. Even a small change in a period of chaos or crisis can produce an enormous impact, and even minor reforms can take on revolutionary significance.** Many schools that are involved in reform projects are implementing very small changes. Some are beginning school 15 minutes earlier or ending 15 minutes later four days a week so that on the fifth day teachers will have an extra hour to plan together. By shifting the way they use a very small amount of time, teachers have been able to create a major change in how they work together, how they plan in teams for student learning, and how they feel about themselves as a professional community in their schools.

14. **Create change in such a way as to reduce the concentration of power and increase respect for rights and interests. By its nature, power leads to corruption. Effective change creates unity only where rights are acknowledged and interests are met.** Groups achieve power by individuals surrendering it. The more power that is passed from individuals to the group, the greater will be the power of the group, but the greater also will be the temptation to use that power to personal advantage. The only protection against the corruption of power lies in the protection of rights, which are limitations on the exercise of power; in the use of collaborative processes to satisfy interests; in the assignment of decision making to small, democratically organized, self-managing teams; in the rotation of leadership based on skill, task, and situation; and in empowering those who do the work to structure how it will be done.

Which principles have you found to be effective in changing your life or your organization? List them here and share them with your colleagues.

_____

_____

_____

_____

Planning Strategically

Here are some of the typical comments employees and managers have made to us about the aimlessness of their organizations and their need for strategic thinking:

It would be helpful for us to create a strategic plan. Having a set of goals and objectives would be useful. When we did it five years ago, it was successful for a few years, but now we don't have an overall plan.

Instead of always putting out fires, we need to create a holistic overview to guide our incremental approach to organizational development.

We should create a plan with objectives that are reachable in the next year. We should make a commitment to a strategic plan with a timetable.

The connection between our hopes and dreams and the lives we live is often tenuous and fragile. We work from crisis to crisis without a strategy, which creates a longing for strategic planning, as in the statements quoted above, or else a manager drafts a plan and controls it, leaving no room for anyone else to join in, participate, or understand how it is supposed to work. One customer service representative we worked with in the midst of a reengineering effort commented on the importance of being strategic:

There is a lack in each department of a clear focus. We have not defined the goals and objectives and what path will meet those objectives. It feels like we are flying by the seat of our pants. Motivation should be more active, but it is hard to be motivated without clear goals. There is a lack of organizational synergy. The organization has a lot of potential. There are a lot of intelligent people who want things to work well, but people seem to be in a static state waiting for someone to tell them what to do.

A friend of ours describes planning as what we do while our lives are going on. We have lots of ideas about how to improve the workplace, but they remain daydreams until we start to become strategic and to plan how we are going to implement them. To be successful, we need to indicate why we need to change, where the change is likely to take us, how it will get us there, and what practical steps we need to take to increase involvement, support, participation, and buy-in throughout the organization.

We received a call from a colleague who was coaching a major consulting and auditing firm through a large scale reengineering project. He needed to know whether to include the vice chair of the company in an envisioning retreat being planned by his senior managers. His concern was that if the vice chair participated, he might suppress others in the group, and if he didn't, he might not support the consensus or decisions of the participants, and disempower them.

Our suggestion was to include the vice chair, since the firm wanted the results of the retreat to have an impact on the organization, but that his presence should not dominate or disempower the group, and that he be clear about his role with the participants. Our strategy was for the group to focus on learning how to be open and honest and have a free exchange of ideas with or without the vice chair present, and for him to focus on learning how to be involved without being dominating or disempowering. Both behaviors were necessary for the organization to truly change. And what better place to start with new behaviors than at an envisioning retreat where these goals could be open for discussion?

Guidelines for Strategic Planning: An Exercise

We have identified a set of guidelines to help you plan more strategically as you work through your own change process. You will see that all these guidelines reflect our point of view about rethinking the way we work. As you go through the list with your own change process in mind, ask yourself or your team members what it would mean to apply each guideline to your organization. For example, what would it mean for you to use the first guideline and start with a blank slate?

In the space provided after each guideline, make notes of the issues you need to address, registering any problems you may have in following these guidelines, ways you might use them to unlock a particularly knotty problem, or how they might apply to your organization's change process.

1. **Start with a blank slate.** All assumptions, past procedures, former structures and systems need to be set aside at the beginning so the change process can make a fresh start. Take nothing for granted. Products, business units, current practices, cultural icons, and work processes should be questioned and justified fully if they are to remain. What are the organizational elements that you want to hold onto and can't question? These may point to old contexts or barriers to change.

    _____

    _____

    _____

2. **Involve everyone who can make a difference.** Everyone, including the janitor and the receptionist, can have an impact on customer service. How can you involve everyone in the process? What would happen if your organization brought everyone together to talk about improvement? Those who feel excluded will generate resistance. Are you leaving people out by assuming they don't have a stake in the outcome?

    _____

    _____

    _____

3. **Identify where you are heading.** Your focus should be on the results you want to produce. The questions to ask are: What outcomes do we want? and How can we produce them? You can answer both questions by creating a vision of where you are heading, identifying the barriers that keep you from getting there, developing strategies to overcome these barriers, and agreeing on action plans that identify who will do what to make these changes happen and when they will begin.

    _____

    _____

    _____

4. **Use a democratic, team-based process.** The people who are directly involved in the work process know the most about the opportunities and obstacles to success in their own jobs and departments. Collaborative team-based consensus on plans for change that flow from a shared vision and arise from brainstormed options will result in a broad base of ownership and commitment that will sustain the change effort over time. What does your organization need to do to create this kind of team process?

    _____

    _____

    _____

5. **Wherever possible, decide by consensus.** Go slower in the beginning to go faster later. Use consensus decision making to create a vision, barriers, strategies, and action plans and do not vote unless absolutely necessary. Try to see disagreement in the group as a sign that you have not yet come up with the best decision. What issues cause the group to get stuck? When does consensus fall apart? Who are the enemies of consensus, and what are their true interests? How can these interests be met?

    _____

    _____

    _____

6. **Share all the information.** There should be no surprises. All people inside an organization should be able to find out everything they want to know about its operations, even about things that are not part of their job or department. The "need to know" should extend to everyone. Are you willing to have an open-book style of management? What information is being hoarded in the organization? How can it be released?

    _____

    _____

    _____

7. **Commit to holistic change.** The entire organization needs to become a part of the change effort. The process from start to finish needs to involve people from all groups at all levels across all organizational lines. Powerful contexts or paradigms and deeply ingrained habits are not going to change without finding their roots in the organization's culture. Do you have a holistic plan that targets these deeper problems and communicates the entire picture of change? Try drawing what needs to change or showing it on a map or chart. What has been left out?

_____

_____

_____

8. **Change all other systems.** All policies and practices within the organization will need to be examined to make certain they support the change effort. For example, what would the consequences be of your organization changing to self-directed teams or to the new paradigm we have described in terms of the following systems and examples?

A. Reward systems
   ♦ Recognition and acknowledgment.
   ♦ Incentives and bonuses.
   ♦ Rewards for identifying and solving problems.

_____

_____

_____

B. Classification systems
   ♦ Job descriptions.
   ♦ Flattened organization charts.
   ♦ Creation and elimination of unnecessary job titles.

_____

_____

_____

C. Pay systems
- Profit participation.
- Raises and promotions.
- Pay for performance/skill/learning, and so on.

_____

_____

_____

D. Work systems
- Decision-making process.
- Autonomy versus dependency.
- Responsibility for outcomes.

_____

_____

_____

E. Management systems
- Performance evaluation.
- Budget development.
- Quality control.

_____

_____

_____

F. Problem-solving and conflict-resolution systems
- Prevention through conflict-resolution systems.
- Problem solving steps, including progressive discipline.
- Mediation and arbitration.

_____

_____

_____

G. Communication systems
- Feedback and evaluation.
- Surveys and assessments.
- Rumor control and informal communication.

_____

_____

_____

H. Cultural systems
- Definitions and meaning.
- Shared values.
- Deference, honesty, and respect for diversity.

_____

_____

_____

I. Other systems that operate in your organization

_____

_____

_____

9. **Make the people as important as the product.** Make sure people feel they are valued, and that the organization does not treat them merely as instruments or producers whose products are more important than they are. What are you doing to let everyone in the organization, as well as their families and significant others, know that without them, there would be no success, no results, no life in the organization?

_____

_____

_____

10. **Make the first steps small and take them together.** Don't begin by trying to change the entire organization at once. Identify some

small, baby steps that will help people feel they can be successful and that the change will make a difference. Identify some "quick hits" that can produce visible change and make life easier for everyone on an immediate basis.

_____

_____

_____

11. **Continuously evaluate and improve both content and process.** Most change efforts focus on the content and ignore the process, and both are often ignored once the change is "over." But in today's world, change is never over. Organizations need to create systems that encourage continuous evaluation and correction. What are some of these systems in your organization? Can you find a way to support the continuous improvement of work processes through ongoing assessments and feedback?

_____

_____

_____

12. **Acknowledge even small successes and reward criticisms and discovery of failure.** Everyone needs to be acknowledged at work, yet our efforts to do so are mostly small and petty. It is hard to overdo rewards and acknowledgments, but what has the most impact is to reward criticism (especially of upper management) and to support the discovery of failure, since these behaviors lead to improvement. How does your organization respond to criticism or failure? Does it encourage learning from mistakes? How? What would you like to be acknowledged for? What rewards might be appropriate for good team behavior? What would make you more willing to criticize or take risks?

_____

_____

_____

13. **Be aware of other factors that influence your organization.** The kind of change that actually takes place in any organization depends not only on the answers to the questions we have posed here but also the emotional and cognitive environment that surrounds the change process: the intentions of those who are leading the change, the strength of the perceived need for change, the length of time people have been waiting for it, the degree of suffering that has been endured in its absence, the ability to think in advance about or plan the change, and the degree of organization that is brought to the change effort. What are some of the environmental factors that could influence change in your organization?

Focusing on Producing Results

Many of the people we work with experience serious burnout, apathy, cynicism, and exhaustion because they feel their efforts have not produced results. They don't see their work lives changing fundamentally or notice people in their organization relating to each other differently. The chaos of the process often leaves them feeling that they are going around and around with the same problems and suggestions, without any clear changes resulting from their efforts. One employee described her experience in these terms:

> We can't get anything done differently. People just continue to behave the same way as before. I think it is because individuals within a particular part of the organization or department or project don't have a clear understanding of the new roles, responsibilities, and expectations for themselves. The change process is unclear. How do we initiate when a change is needed? What force is needed to make it work? How do we take the overall strategy and put it into our particular jobs?

We developed the following worksheet to help you focus on how to build forward momentum so as to produce results. It has proven useful to us in a variety of settings: with teams of teacher leaders who were part of a national project to transform the ways children learn in schools; with self-directed teams in corporate settings planning new customer service initiatives; and with a team of hospital administrators, doctors, and nurses who were reorganizing the leadership of their health care facility.

The worksheet that follows also provides a framework for rethinking how you might change your own work life to humanize it by shifting the paradigm in which you work. Please use it as a tool to see where you are going and how you want to get there. Some of the questions may not be useful, and others may occur to you along the way. Please adapt it to your own needs.

Worksheet for Results: An Exercise

1. What is your vision for the future? What do you want?

    _____

    _____

    _____

2. What are the values you want to express? What is important to you?

    _____

    _____

    _____

3. What are your goals? What do you want to accomplish in the next two to three years?

    _____

    _____

    _____

4. What experiences, skills, and needs do you bring from your own background, and how do they combine with the resources brought by other team members?

    _____

    _____

    _____

5. What barriers could keep you from achieving your vision? Are these barriers isolated or systemic?

_____

_____

_____

6. What solutions can you see to your problems? Are the solutions solitary or developmental?

_____

_____

_____

7. What is the time required to respond to the problems and implement the solutions? Is it short term or long term?

_____

_____

_____

8. Who needs to be involved to make your plan succeed?

_____

_____

_____

9. Who can veto or block the plan's success?

_____

_____

_____

10. What communication systems will allow people to talk or listen so that they can support your plan?

_____

_____

_____

11. What tasks need to be accomplished? What is the order of their priority?

_____

_____

_____

12. What size group will work best for each task?

_____

_____

_____

13. What group process will work best for each task?

_____

_____

_____

14. What groups need to coalesce in order for the plan to be successful?

_____

_____

_____

15. What are the likely sources of internal and external conflict? What are the likely sources of resolution?

_____

_____

_____

16. How can issues or potential solutions be reframed to reduce unnecessary conflict?

_____

_____

_____

17. What problem-solving and conflict-resolution structures would help prevent, reduce, manage, and resolve potential conflicts before they become damaging?

_____

_____

_____

18. How can discussion, understanding, and participation in solving the problem be broadened?

_____

_____

_____

19. How can the solution be legitimized or made understandable to people who oppose it?

_____

_____

_____

20. How can you keep interest and involvement alive?

_____

_____

_____

21. How can you track milestones and provide status reports?

_____

_____

_____

22. What are the results you have produced and how do you evaluate your success?

_____

_____

_____

23. How can networking and group learning be improved?

_____

_____

_____

24. How can you expand or replicate your successes without imposing your model on others?

_____

_____

_____

25. How will you celebrate success? Who will be rewarded?

_____

_____

_____

26. What have you learned from the change process so far? How could it help you become more effective the next time you change?

_____

_____

_____

Completing this exercise should give you the information you need to start a major change initiative. Your answers alone are not enough. We suggest you photocopy this form and distribute it to team members, colleagues, partners, and co-workers so you can compare your answers and gain perspective on what others need before you begin. These answers will allow you to develop a strategic plan that will guide you through the change process.

Humanizing the Change Process

Philip Jackson, who for many years was dean of the School of Education at the University of Chicago, wrote about his experiences during a sabbatical year in which he sat at the back of classrooms observing teachers he had interviewed. In his book, *Life in Classrooms,* he noted that the most important element in determining a teacher's behavior was whether the children were in the classroom. That is, the teacher created lesson plans, set up displays, organized activities, and decorated the classroom, alone and without students present. But when children came into the picture, everything changed: the lesson plans were adjusted; the displays were mussed and used; the activities were turned around; and the decorations were rearranged, added to, or torn down.

We have seen the same dynamic happen in reengineering processes. Careful plans are made; detailed blueprints are drawn; high expectations are set for the organization; visions, goals, and strategies are charted elegantly, and the whole change plan seems brilliant. But it all gets messed up once people become involved, and all the beautiful plans remain unfulfilled.

So in case you are starting to become enamored of your visions, theories, and plans, here are four basic lessons we have learned about what happens when people become involved in the change process. We hope these lessons will help you understand how others in your organization may respond to the change process. Learning these lessons may prepare you to deal with them proactively so they do not paralyze or sabotage the process.

LESSON #1: CHANGE INDUCES FEELINGS OF LOSS

Certainty and comfort are always threatened when we make fundamental changes because, as Machiavelli recognized in the opening quotation to this chapter, change requires transition from a known order to an uncertain disorder, and for this reason it produces resistance—even when it is clear that the purpose of the change is only to create a more successful kind of order.

Elizabeth Kubler-Ross in her classic book *On Death and Dying*, described the stages many of us experience when we face any kind of loss. We have observed that her model also describes the way many of us process organizational change. Her research suggests that when loss occurs, we often experience the following emotions: denial, bargaining, anger, depression, and acceptance. One of our clients suggested we add "forgiveness" as a sixth stage, while another suggested adding "celebration."

Whatever the number of stages or how we define them, when teams, individuals, groups, and departments are not allowed time to experience the full range of these reactions, the change process gets stalled, because the feelings associated with it have been suppressed, rather than communicated and released. A lack of adequate completion or closure regarding the past is one of the greatest barriers to acceptance and forward movement in generating organizational change.

We once worked for an organization that was in the midst of far-reaching changes and had gone from 18 small, independent manufacturing units to a single centralized operation. In the process, many jobs had been lost, roles were changed, reporting relationships revised, and locations of service centers moved so that many people had to relocate. The director who initiated these changes knew that to be successful he had to give people time and a way to process their loss, to understand the changes, and to move on.

He and his deputy traveled to each site and spent many days meeting in small groups with each separate constituency, briefing clients, listening to concerns, speaking to problems, and allowing an open and occasionally uncomfortable expression of emotion. There were tears in some cases, painful confrontations, and some messy meetings. But in the end, at the conclusion of the process, the organization was on the road to healing. Two reactions to this experience came out in our interviews with the participants:

Through the process of working through the feelings we have gained the ability to feel that we have a real mission that has lots of support at all levels. We were very diverse before—18 . . . groups, with everybody doing their own thing. The chance to be effective has really grown with the change.

Creating a new organizational structure from many separate structures was a political nightmare but we did it. Talking it through really paid off in the people factor, and also the fact that we cut overhead. We saved $30,000,000 for the business in the bargain. We helped the bottom line on profit sharing for all the employees and helped the bottom line on peoples' understanding and caring along the way.

Part of humanizing the workplace, in our minds, is allowing people to experience their emotions without being considered unprofessional. Fewer disruptions take place when we release our emotions than when we suppress them. We often want our managers and leaders to be emotionless, largely because we know that disasters take place more readily when we combine emotions with power. If we surrender our power, we are able to experience our emotions and release them, rather than keeping them bottled up where they may leak out in subtle and dangerous ways.

LESSON #2: CHANGE ALWAYS CREATES RESISTANCE

We all know people whose first and automatic response to any proposed change is *NO!* We may actually be this kind of person. Even if the change has been anticipated, wished for, planned, and dreamt about, it can still create anxiety, unease, and resistance. Remember the first day of school when you were abandoned by your parents and left with a stranger, your teacher? You may have been excited to start your adventure in the world, yet at the same time resistant to the changes school would bring to your life.

Retirement is another example of the difficulties created by change. Many people look forward to the end of their work and the beginning of "free time." Yet the statistics on retirement reveal that many people who retire either die or become seriously ill shortly after achieving what they have longed for all their working lives. Why? Because the change was not planned for by gradually increasing the amount of nonwork time, but by going "cold turkey" after a lifetime's addiction to work; because many retirees never separated their personal identities from their workplace personae. When the work died, they died with it. Those who make the change gradually or continue to work at something are less upset when retirement happens and better able to cope with the change.

As you consider the changes you would like to make in your work life, notice whether you might also be feeling resistant about actually starting the change process. People naturally want to protect their jobs as they are, and personally identify with paradigms that are familiar, even when they are outmoded. If this is your reaction, your job may be too important in defining how you see yourself. Who you are and how you value yourself should not depend on your job. Our sense of ourselves should *transcend* and find expression in our work, not the other way around.

This deep, personal identification we have with our jobs and our inability to find other ways of defining ourselves are one source of the pain, illness, and depression that occurs on the job, as well as after retirement. When we ask managers or employees in our trainings to create visions for their personal lives after retirement, they often talk about volunteering time in community service, trying teaching, going back to their first careers, learning painting or carpentry, writing a book, opening a small restaurant, or creating their own business. Envisioning helps make the transition to retirement less traumatic, and is a useful technique in any change process because it refocuses attention from the loss of our past to the gains that can occur in our future.

In the current work environment, as layoffs continue and many people have to discover new jobs or work roles, the loss of job identification is becoming more common. Nearly every organization we know of is considering major changes in how people work, which also requires us to change the titles and job descriptions we have used to identify ourselves. The resistance and upset that accompany these changes are also triggered when people are asked to change the *way* they work, which leads us to lesson 3.

LESSON #3: PEOPLE TAKE CHANGE PERSONALLY, AND INTERPRET IT THROUGH THE DETAILS

When a change is instituted or suggested, those who are affected by it inevitably ask three questions: What does it mean to me? What does it mean to me? What does it mean to me? You can present an inspiring vision for the future, you can promise that the changes will produce wonderful results, you can find creative ways of serving your clients more effectively and profoundly, and the response may still be: Will I lose my parking space? Will I have to change my schedule and miss my van-pool ride? What does this mean about which work space I get?

Until these seemingly minor, insignificant questions have been answered satisfactorily and in detail, it will be difficult to generate enthusiasm, buy-in, support, or understanding of what the change is about. Once these questions have been recognized as basic and practical and been answered, the people they affect can start to listen for the first time and open themselves to learning about the visionary concepts, substantive content, or contextual shifts that are being proposed.

When one of our client organizations moved to self-directed teams, the early focus of its employees had nothing to do with the importance of the team concept or the vision of the organization or learning new "people skills." Their first major focus was on where the team cubicles would be located! Once people knew where they would be sitting and who would be next to them, they could give their full attention to these "larger" concerns.

If we ignore any of these lessons of change, we can become stymied very quickly. Beginning the change process by acknowledging and experiencing the loss, dealing with feelings of resistance and identity confusion, and meeting the concrete, everyday needs of the people who are going through the change process are the best strategies to use. As you try to change your organization, humanize your workplace, or simply improve your work life, keep these alternative ways of participating in change in mind—not as judgments, but as alternatives that can be chosen at any and every moment in the process.

Becoming Effective Change Agents

We recommend to most organizations that they begin the change process by identifying an internal team of "change agents" from throughout the organization whose job it is to reinforce organizational learning, coach individuals and teams, and translate the lessons learned during the change into day-to-day operations. These informal in-house leaders play a significant role in bringing the change to fruition. They remain involved when the outsiders and consultants leave. They know what is needed and appropriate because they live it every day. They have access and credibility with their colleagues and will see more than outsiders who can only discover whatever people feel safe enough to reveal. By creating such a team, the external change agent leaves behind resources to support lasting change.

Taking on the role of a change agent may seem like a demanding responsibility. But if you have stayed with us this far, you may have already assumed this role. You can experience a tremendous payoff by taking responsibility for change. There are enormous personal lessons to learn, new skills to develop, honest feedback to absorb, and genuine achievements to savor. While risks are also involved, the rewards outweigh them in the long run.

We worked with several members of an internal change team who felt they had learned a great deal by being change agents and by advising and facilitating self-directed teams inside their own organization. They told us:

I now watch my tendency to dominate in meetings. I tend to have very strong and decisive ideas and to voice them very quickly. This immediately stifles everyone else from even trying to come up with their own ideas. I've learned that even in situations where I believe my own idea will likely or possibly be the group's eventual decision, I'll wait and give others a chance. It will encourage others not to look for me to have the ideas. I try to give others an opportunity to lead and participate in the meeting.

I'm getting better at not over-committing my time. I tend to squeeze in more meetings than are reasonable and therefore to be late for most of them.

I am trying to display a heightened awareness and sensitivity to the issues people will face in the transition. I am especially focusing on developing my communication and negotiation skills.

My role as a coach has helped me to think in a broader sense how teams are affecting the organization and company and how I can contribute. I find that I am questioning more, especially the traditional rules and processes. And I tend to challenge my assumptions about constraints and areas of control. It looks like my tendency is probably to impose more constraints than really exist.

These testimonies to the personal growth that takes place when employees voluntarily assume the role of leader, facilitator, recorder, coach, or mediator point to the personal advantages of becoming a change agent and an actor in the drama of transformation. Whether you embrace this role formally and anoint yourself a Super Change Agent or work in your own quiet way, the following words of caution and advice, some of which were suggested by Ozzie Bermant, may be useful as you venture out into the world of change.

I. **Walk your talk.** As Tom Peters and Bob Waterman advocate, be consistent. Practice what you preach to others and let them see you actually do it when it counts. If you can't, let them hear you acknowledge it, learn from it, and try to do better next time.

2. **Don't drink the water.** Don't let the negativity that affects your organization get you down. Don't get trapped in the self-defeating, apathetic, or cynical culture that is a byproduct of the old paradigm and is intended to discourage participation in change.

3. **Fix systems rather than people.** Rather than focusing on changing people, change the systems that shape how they behave and relate to one another. Both problems and solutions have systemic roots, and the change process is easier when you concentrate on the ways a system rewards negative behaviors, rather than on the personalities of the people who have been trapped by that system.

4. **Changing yourself automatically changes others.** You are also a part of the system. If you change, everyone else has to change as well. People will need to reexamine how they relate to you, and how they deal with one another when they are around you. Changing some of the ways an organization operates results in changing the system as a whole.

5. **There is no such thing as neutral observation.** Just looking at a problem begins the process of changing it. If you observe a problem or a system long enough, if you begin to call attention to it, the solutions start to arise.

6. **Look with peripheral vision; use a floodlight as well as a spotlight.** Look at all aspects of the situation. What is directly in front of you may not be the entire story. Use a floodlight to see the surrounding area, and a spotlight to zero in on the specifics. Change has to be global and systemic, but it also has to reach the smallest level of work to be complete and successful. Often it is the smallest details that make or break a change effort.

7. **Float like a butterfly; sting like a bee.** Be open and flexible and at the same time focused and hard hitting. Stay on your toes so you don't get knocked over by problems. Be deeply honest about what is not working in your organization, but focus on the problems and do not make the people wrong, or get stuck on a single solution.

8. **Search for preventative opportunities.** Preventing a problem is easier than solving it repeatedly. Head off conflict with

communication and conciliation before it is required. Design systems that will prevent problems you know you are going to face, or that give you an early warning sign that something is not going right.

9. **Go slow to go fast.** Use consensus as a process. Make sure everyone is included and feels heard. Don't try to force decision making when you run into difficulty. Stop and recognize that you are stuck. Look at the interests of each side in an effort to improve ideas or proposals before moving forward. Take a little longer to make it right.

10. **Think of conflict as an opportunity for growth, improvement, and learning.** Do not suppress conflicts, but look for what they can teach you. Find the new paradigm to which the conflict may be pointing. Try to take the issues to a deeper level and see the conflict as an indication that you need to improve the way things are working, or the level of skill you are able to bring to solving the problem.

11. **Change "me versus them" into "us versus it."** Be hard on the problem and soft on the people. Shift the focus of the conflict from personalities and people to problem solving and organizational growth. See others not as enemies, but as allies, and they will be more likely to respond with support than with self-defense or counterattack.

12. **Don't stand between addicts and their dope.** A frontal assault does not always work as well as an end run, particularly if you are dealing with someone who is addicted to their problems or to their power or to their job. Model a different way of approaching problems by seeing them as challenges and opportunities. Don't fight battles over false issues or coerce people into doing things your way. The best strategy is to be honest about what you think is really happening and let each person decide on the right response for themselves.

13. **Be optimistic in your heart and realistic in your head.** Be open to your heart's message and your mind's logic. Hope for success and recognize that it might not happen. Look for the intrinsic potential that is in each human being, but do not ignore their

weaknesses. Use your heart to affirm and accept and your mind to understand and strategize.

14. **Let go. Give up your expectations.** If you expect the change to take place in a certain way or for others to adopt your personal ideas or solutions, you will probably be disappointed. Be open to discovering the enormous potential that can happen when a team effort occurs. Allow the results of the change process to instruct you. The greater the openness, the greater the potential for change.

15. **Different strokes for different folks.** You cannot mandate the things that matter to people. The same solutions do not work for everyone. Local variability is the rule rather than the exception, which is why most pilot projects work while most models don't. Allow room for diversity and try to see difference as a source of strength.

16. **Change always takes longer than planned.** Double your planning time and still don't expect to make your target. Renegotiate deadlines as you progress. Change takes whatever time it actually needs. How long it takes is based not on how soon you would like the change to be completed, but on how soon all the actual requirements are able to come into place.

17. **Learn from each other.** Change efforts need to be coordinated, and diverse constituencies need to be united in order to succeed. Your greatest teachers will not be change gurus, but other students. Networks, cross-training, mentoring, and peer counseling are highly successful means of allowing each person to be both a teacher and a student.

18. **Don't dominate the process—leave room for others.** You don't need to control the process or solve all the problems yourself. The best solutions are those people create for themselves because that is often the only way they can own them. Full involvement and the ability to choose between alternatives fuels the change process and helps develop leaders. Remember, leadership *adores* a vacuum. Accountability for results does not have to mean conformity or domination.

19. **Don't look for magic wands.** Most of what actually happens during a change process is discovered as it unfolds. The chaos that

is involved in any complicated change means that it is inherently unpredictable. There are no formulas or blueprints to follow or guarantees to be had. Following someone else's blueprint will lead you in some direction other than your own.

20. **Don't be afraid of success.** Do not let your self-doubts or fear of the unknown get in your way. Allow yourself to be successful by trying to implement the changes you want. Recognize that individual efforts *can* make a difference, and that small changes often produce larger ones. If you are willing to take the risk of beginning, you can actually achieve your dream and see your goals realized. Let your fears dissolve by starting with small steps, for example, by talking to your co-workers and deciding to act together.

SEVEN

Seeing Conflict as Opportunity

We have thought of peace as passive and war as the active way of living. The opposite is true. War is not the most strenuous life. It is a kind of rest cure compared to the task of reconciling our differences. . . . From War to Peace is not from the strenuous to the easy existence; it is from the futile to the effective, from the stagnant to the active, from the destructive to the creative way of life. . . . The world will be regenerated by the people who rise above these passive ways and heroically seek, by whatever hardship, by whatever toil, the methods by which people can agree.

MARY PARKER FOLLETT, 1868–1933

Conflict Is Everywhere

A visionary leader has great plans to transform her service organization from a hierarchy to self-directed teams. Her boss is threatened by this development and thinks this visionary lacks the skills to succeed in the new environment, so he demands high levels of detailed information, constant reporting, and tries to control each step in the process, modeling not empowerment but command and control. Employees see their two leaders locked in conflict about the future of their organization and decide not to participate in the change process.

A new male teacher is assigned by his principal to join a team that has been functioning well for several years. The other members of the team are all women. They work so well together, they often finish each others' sentences. The new member has been successful as a loner and feels rejected by the team's closeness. He immediately tells the other teachers that he doesn't believe in "all this team stuff" and doesn't respect any of them as colleagues. The entire effort gets bogged down in conflict.

Two deputy directors of a large bank vie for the attention and support of their director. They each come from different family backgrounds. He is the oldest of six, the only male, and often responsible for telling his other siblings how to behave. She is a middle child, used to confiding in her two brothers and being their pal and playmate, and resents being bossed around by men. The conflicts between them even extend to arguments over how they should fight, and their boss, an only child, played them off against each other.

These stories are only a few of the millions that could be told about conflict in the workplace. Most of the organizations we observe are *riddled* with unresolved conflict. Disputes between employees and managers, managers and supervisors, employees and the public, secretaries and bosses, doctors and nurses, union representatives and labor relations departments, manufacturing and shipping, people who are creative and people who are practical, those who are "mellow" and those who are "up tight," those who talk but don't listen and those who listen but don't talk—all produce disputes that form a regular, ongoing part of nearly every work environment.

One member of a leadership team in an entrepreneurial sales organization described his experience with a conflict that nearly ruined the company:

The climate here needs to change drastically, and we need to learn how to respect people and listen to each other. Process skills are greatly needed. When we get tired and stressed we lose it and blow up with each other and cause a lot of damage. The customers are not getting served, and neither are we.

We need to listen to one another more and allow time for other people's ideas to be understood. This is not a Ping-Pong game, although most of the time it feels that way, and I feel like the ball! I'm leaving the company if they don't stop it.

A survey conducted by the American Management Association, responded to by 116 CEO's, 76 vice presidents, and 66 middle managers, revealed that these individuals spent at least *24 percent* of their time resolving conflicts at work; that conflict resolution had become increasingly important over the last 10 years; and that conflict resolution was either more important or equally as important as planning, communication, motivation, and decision making.

The principle causes of conflict within the organizations that were surveyed were seen as misunderstanding, communication failure, personality clashes, value and goal differences, substandard performance, differences over method, responsibility issues, lack of cooperation, authority issues, frustration and irritability, competition for limited resources, and noncompliance with rules and policies.

Yet these are not the only causes of conflict, and in most of the workplaces we have worked in, 24 percent is a low-end figure, particularly when minor everyday disputes are included. If we consider that conflict often reveals itself first in rumors and gossip, then in apathy and cynicism, and only later in resistance and sabotage, the figures for the amount of management time spent trying to resolve all of these conflicts is probably 50 percent or higher.

Conflict not only wastes huge amounts of time but wastes money, energy, and morale as well. For most organizations, it is not simply the time spent on grievances, arbitration, litigation, and arguments that is the problem, but the time people waste in petty gossip talking about what the other person did or said; in thinking about what to say or do in response; in personal leave, sick days, and absenteeism due to anger, fear, or shame; in lost production time and deteriorated morale; and in countless petty distractions. When we add up all the time wasted in unproductive conflicts, the costs are overwhelming.

If we are right about the changing paradigm of work, a more humanized approach should produce better results in responding to conflicts than the old paradigm did. One of the most difficult issues for us to handle in a humanized way is conflict. If we can find better ways of responding to the chronic conflicts that plague our workplaces, we will be able to use the time, money, energy, and morale that is presently being wasted to encourage growth and organizational learning.

Conflict in Our Lives: An Exercise

As we begin our exploration of the ways organizations handle conflict, take a moment to reflect on the conflicts in your own life. Try to recall the conflicts you faced or observed last week by completing the chart below. As you raise your awareness of the number and variety of conflicts in your work environment, you may notice areas of conflict that have always remained hidden or beneath the surface. Now that you are looking for conflicts, you may suddenly see them in places you never suspected. You may also find that some of your unexplained exhaustion, frustration, poor health, and dissatisfaction with work is caused by unaddressed conflicts that are preventing you from being effective.

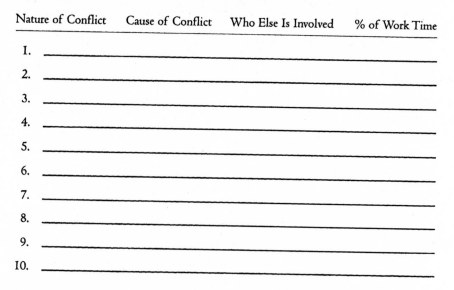

Nature of Conflict	Cause of Conflict	Who Else Is Involved	% of Work Time
1.			
2.			
3.			
4.			
5.			
6.			
7.			
8.			
9.			
10.			

How We Respond to Conflict

To understand the role conflict plays in our organizations and why we respond to it as we do, we need to start thinking of it differently. We have addressed the need to change our contexts and paradigms of work, but we also need to look at the contexts and paradigms we have created about the conflicts we experience, because they are often linked together.

When we work with organizations that are experiencing chronic conflict, we often begin our sessions by asking, "What do you do or feel when you are involved in conflict?" The responses we get most often include getting angry, wanting to run away, giving in, crying, feeling ashamed or sad, and withdrawing. These responses are negative because they leave us feeling powerless or angry and because they do not address the problem.

In its negative form, conflict saps energy and makes achieving our goal far more difficult. It decreases productivity, reduces morale, prevents cooperation, aggravates minor differences, polarizes points of view, encourages irresponsible behavior, generates suspicion and mistrust, obstructs communication, increases tension and stress, obscures vision, and results in the loss of valuable human resources. While most of us recognize from personal experience that conflict can be counterproductive, we also know that it can help us clarify our goals, relieve our tensions, and open communications.

While we generally think of conflict negatively, as something to be avoided at all costs, we know that many personal and organizational benefits flow from conflict, including change, learning, growth, deeper understanding, greater intimacy in relationships, and the possibility of a resolution that actually solves the underlying problem. None of these are possible when our only responses are negative.

In the workplace, our immediate responses to conflict are most often negative, rather than positive, and include the following:

1. **Ignore it.** Withdrawal, avoidance, or retreat from conflict is perhaps the most common workplace response, because involvement in any conflict is potentially job threatening. This response not only leaves the underlying problems unresolved, it often creates greater problems through neglect and encourages irresponsibility toward others.

2. **Dodge it.** Referring the problem to someone else is no different from ignoring it. Nor is it particularly useful to blame others for the conflict. The underlying issues cannot be addressed when it is always "somebody else's problem" or fault.

3. **Cover it up.** Most managers without training in conflict resolution first try to smooth over the conflict, generally by "oiling the squeaky wheel" or suppressing the discontent. Neither of these strategies helps in the long run and often increases the level of conflict.

4. **Decide it yourself.** The old paradigm made managers into dispute resolvers, but did not provide them with the skills to do so collaboratively, and it became customary for managers to simply bulldoze the conflict and resolve it *for* the participants. But resolution by fiat is dangerous and frequently counterproductive, as the manager cannot know all the facts and may later appear foolish or stupid or incur the resentment and hostility of either or both sides.

5. **Litigate it.** Another common method is to let the dispute proceed to grievance, arbitration, or court. The outcome then will be a win/lose result in which one party will suffer at the hands of the other, while the truth more often lies somewhere in between. In court, both parties surrender their control over outcomes to some third party who does not understand the problem as well as they do, and there is rarely a chance to discover what is really going on behind the conflict.

6. **Give in to it.** Accommodation may reduce the conflict temporarily, but it leaves an aftertaste of resentment or resistance and does not resolve the underlying issues, which simply generate new conflicts until a solution is found.

7. **Compromise it.** A more effective technique is to identify the parties' interests, search for compromise solutions, and negotiate outcomes that convert the outcome to one where, if there is to be a loss, it is borne equally.

8. **Resolve it together.** The most effective methods for resolving conflict are informal, collaborative problem solving and mediation in which the parties themselves, sometimes with the assistance of someone outside the conflict, discuss their problems, communicate with each other, and negotiate mutually agreeable, voluntary solutions to the underlying problems that created the conflict.

Most organizational cultures have a preferred way of responding to conflict. Which of the strategies we've described are used most often in your organization? Which strategies do you use most often? In the exercise you completed above in which you recorded conflicts in your workplace, which of these strategies did you or other employees or managers use to respond to the conflicts you identified? How successful were these strategies?

Conflict and Communication: A Self-Assessment Exercise

We are often unaware of our own behaviors when we are in conflict. Our responses are usually in reaction to others, and we do not stop and think about the way we are responding. What is your usual pattern for handling conflict? What do you need to do to be more effective in responding to it? How can you maximize the collaborative and positive approaches to conflict and minimize the negative ones? Try filling out the following questionnaire on the next page to give yourself some feedback.

When you have completed the questionnaire, find a partner or a colleague who knows you well. Review your responses and ask what their perceptions are of your behavior. Encourage them to give you an honest appraisal. You are in this process to learn, and their feedback can be a valuable source of information for your growth.

Alternative Definitions of Conflict

Since we know that organizational conflict can lead to positive results, what prevents us from responding to it positively and collaboratively? One answer is that we believe in a paradigm of conflict that defines it as a negative experience. Most of our negative paradigms of conflict are responses to some of the behaviors we described above, which all of us engage in.

What follows is a set of alternative definitions of conflict, which we have drawn from our experiences in mediating a wide variety of organizational and interpersonal disputes. They are designed to stimulate your thinking and to give you a new way of looking at the conflicts you may be experiencing at work. As you review these categories, see if you

When I am in conflict, I . . .	Need to Do More	Need to Do Less	Do OK	Don't Know How I Do
1. Withhold judgment.				
2. Deal with present behavior instead of bringing up the past.				
3. Pay attention to nonverbal cues.				
4. Use "I" messages; i.e., describe my own feelings, instead of the other person's.				
5. Avoid blaming.				
6. Am open with my feelings and opinions.				
7. Am careful of using jargon "trigger" words that aggravate the conflict.				
8. Withhold information.				
9. Restate or paraphrase what I hear.				
10. Listen for feelings and reflect them back to the sender.				
11. Ask open-ended questions.				
12. Try to control the other person.				
13. Am able to concede points without hostility and employ statements such as "You may be right."				
14. Avoid judging motives or making assumptions about others.				
15. Avoid giving advice.				
16. Try to put myself in the other person's place.				
17. Recognize and legitimize emotions before dealing with content.				
18. Clear up as many assumptions as possible.				
19. Focus on points of agreement before clarifying points for negotiation.				
20. Use humor to ease tension.				
21. Am honest about what I contributed to the conflict.				
22. Avoid becoming defensive.				
23. Use empathy or role reversal.				
24. Focus on interests rather than positions.				
25. Look for completion and closure.				

can think of an example of a conflict you have experienced or observed
in the past six months that illustrates the category. In the space provided,
indicate the conflict you have identified and explain why it may be
possible to approach or think of it differently.

1. Conflict represents a lack of skill or experience at being able to
    handle a particular kind of behavior.

    _____

    _____

    _____

2. Conflict is the voice of a new context or paradigm, a call for
    change in a system that has outlived its usefulness.

    _____

    _____

    _____

3. Conflict is a sign of a lack of collaboration, teamwork, and
    community.

    _____

    _____

    _____

4. Conflict is the sound made by the cracks in a system, by
    contradictory forces that are trying to coexist in a single organization.

    _____

    _____

    _____

5. Conflict reflects an ignorance of our essential interconnectedness,
    of the cooperation that allows our work to produce results.

    _____

    _____

    _____

6. Conflict is a lack of acceptance of ourselves that we have projected onto others, a way of blaming someone else for what we perceive as failures in our own work, of diverting attention from our mistakes.

    _____

    _____

    _____

7. Conflict is a boundary violation, a failure to value or recognize our own integrity or the personal space of others.

    _____

    _____

    _____

8. Conflict reflects a need to support or maintain a false image of who we really are.

    _____

    _____

    _____

9. Conflict is a way of obtaining acknowledgment, sympathy, or support by casting ourselves as the victim of some evildoer.

    _____

    _____

    _____

10. Conflict is the continued pursuit of our own false expectations, the desire to hold on to unrealistic fantasies.

    _____

    _____

    _____

11. Conflict is a lack of appreciation for the subtlety in what someone else is saying.

_____

_____

_____

12. Conflict is a product of what is not communicated, of secrets, confusion, and coverup.

_____

_____

_____

13. Conflict is a lack of effectiveness or clarity in communicating what we feel, think, or want.

_____

_____

_____

14. Conflict is a way of opposing someone who represents the parent or sibling with whom we have not yet resolved our relationship.

_____

_____

_____

15. Conflict is the inability to say good-bye, a refusal to let go of something that is dead or dying.

_____

_____

_____

16. Conflict is a way of being negatively intimate when positive intimacy has become impossible.

_____

_____

_____

17. Conflict is the antagonistic voice of half of a paradox, enigma, duality, polarity, or contradiction.

_____

_____

_____

18. Conflict is the fear of difference, diversity, or opposition.

_____

_____

_____

19. Conflict is a request for authenticity, empathy, emotional honesty, acknowledgment, communication, understanding, and a better relationship.

_____

_____

_____

20. Conflict is an opportunity for organizational learning, growth, and change.

_____

_____

_____

The common element in each of these definitions is that they have little or nothing to do with the behavior of our opponent. Our conflicts begin and end with us and with the contexts and paradigms we inhabit. Each of these alternative definitions opens a window of awareness, points to a strategy for resolution, and offers us a unique and powerful opportunity for personal and organizational transformation that depends on our openness and capacity to listen to voices that are not our own. As you reflect on the examples you listed, notice the implications for your own behavior, your own ideas about conflict, and your responsibility for the conflicts about which you are a part.

Conflict Resolution Strategies

You may be wondering how you *should* respond to conflict? What are the strategies that seem to work? We are often asked to give simple solutions for all our conflicts. Unfortunately, we have no such magic remedy. Instead, we have discovered from our experience with the conflicts in our own lives, as mediators, and from observing many clients and colleagues through the years, that individuals and organizations need to use a variety of conflict resolution strategies that depend on their goals or concerns, and on the nature of the conflict. Our basic choices when we are in conflict are:

1. **Avoidance or nonengagement** in which we end up avoiding involvement and feeling isolated and alone, and not becoming part of the organization.

2. **Accommodation or surrender** in which we give up or give in to a superior force, obey its rules, and end up feeling used; we obey the organization's rules but passively subvert them whenever we can.

3. **Aggression, hostility, or open opposition** in which we find a powerful strategy, but it is a strategy that is competitive and pitted against others, and we often end up feeling negative, embittered, hostile, and petty.

4. **Compromise, negotiation, or give-and-take** in which we end up feeling somewhat satisfied and somewhat dissatisfied, with a contractual or legalistic outcome that is based on balancing conflicting interests.

5. **Collaboration or partnership** in which we end up feeling empowered and connected with others and generate a humanistic organization that operates synergistically.

Each of these strategies is useful under different circumstances. The following list explains when you might choose one approach to conflict over another.

1. **Avoiding or dodging the conflict.**
   - When an issue seems trivial.
   - When one has no power or can't change.
   - When the damage due to conflict outweighs its benefits.
   - In order to cool down, reduce tensions, or regain composure.
   - When the need to gather information outweighs the need to make an immediate decision.
   - When others can resolve the conflict more effectively.
   - When the issue is tangential or symptomatic.

2. **Accommodating or giving in to the conflict.**
   - When one is wrong, or to show one is reasonable.
   - When the issue is more important to others, or to establish good will.
   - To build up credits.
   - When one is outmatched or losing.
   - To preserve harmony or avoid disruption.
   - To help subordinates develop by letting them learn from their mistakes.

3. **Aggression or engaging in the conflict.**
   - To achieve quick decisive action.
   - In an emergency.
   - To enforce unpopular rules or discipline.
   - When the issues are vital and one knows one is right.
   - To protect oneself against people who take advantage of noncompetitive behavior.

4. **Compromise or negotiating the conflict.**
   - When your goals are moderately important.
   - When opponents with equal power are strongly committed to mutually exclusive goals.
   - To achieve a temporary settlement of complex issues.
   - To arrive at expedient solutions under time pressure.
   - As a backup when competition or collaboration fails.

5. **Collaborating or using teamwork in the conflict.**
    - To find an integrative solution when both sides find it hard to compromise.
    - When the objective is to learn.
    - To merge insights that come from different perspectives.
    - When long-range solutions are required.
    - To gain commitment by consensual decision-making.
    - To empower one or both participants.
    - To work through hard feelings.
    - To model cooperative solutions for others.
    - To solve problems between people who work closely together.
    - To end the conflict rather than paper it over.
    - To improve morale.
    - To increase motivation and productivity.
    - When a team effort is required.
    - When creative solutions are needed.
    - When all other methods fail.

(Source: Thomas-Kilman Instrument)

These alternative strategies may open different paths toward resolution for you. You may now see that if you can analyze the conflict and know your goals, you can step back from the battle long enough to choose a strategy and become far more effective at resolving it. Practice some of these strategies. Try them out, based on the circumstances and what you want to accomplish. Notice that you can use different strategies in different ways and can expand your repertoire so you feel comfortable with several strategies.

It is relatively easy for most of us to avoid, accommodate, get aggressive, or even find a compromise. What we do not know how to do nearly as well is to *join* our opponent in a mutual search for collaborative solutions. However, this alternative is the one solution that leads directly to the humanization we have been discussing, and that opens the greatest opportunity for growth, learning, change, and all the other benefits of full resolution.

A clear relationship exists between the way we handle conflict, the way we respond to change, and the kind of organization or community we end up creating as a result. Each of the approaches to conflict listed above corresponds to a set of attitudes toward the change process, and these attitudes and styles correspond to different varieties or levels of community. These patterns manifest themselves on a small scale in families and teams; on a larger scale in organizations, workplaces, and neighborhoods; and on a still larger scale in nation-states. The ways we choose to approach conflict and change therefore result in vastly different kinds of social interactions, relationships, and organization or association, as can be seen in the following chart:

Conflict Style	Attitude to Change	Form of Organization
Avoidance	Apathy and cynicism	Isolated organization
Accommodation	Obedience and resistance	Pseudo organization
Aggression	Reaction and sabotage	Negative organization
Compromise	Formal compliance	Bureaucratic organization
Collaboration	Ownership and affirmation	Humanistic organization

This chart demonstrates that the five basic approaches to conflict, change, and organization have something in common and that we can identify a set of predictable group outcomes to how we respond to conflict.

Conflict as Opportunity

We can now see that the new paradigm of the humanized, inclusive, empowering workplace, when applied to conflict, is the only one that ends in collaboration, that generates a positive outcome to the conflict, or that allows the conflict to become a source of organizational learning. If you look at your own conflicts this way, a number of possibilities will open up for you. If you can think about the way you approach conflict in the same manner that you think about the way you play tennis or cook a meal, in other words as a *skill* rather than as a fate or a judgment, you will begin to focus on becoming more skillful and increase your opportunities to learn from the conflicts in your life.

Conflict is an opportunity to learn how to avoid the reptile brain's "fight or flight" responses of avoidance, accommodation, and aggression, and to look for an alternative that promotes compromise, or preferably collaboration. The following skills are useful in responding to conflict collaboratively and in turning it into an opportunity:

1. **Listen actively.** The way to begin a collaborative outcome is by listening. "Active listening" techniques are based on the realization that conflict is fundamentally a request for communication. One of the purposes of our anger is to get through to the other person so our adversary can finally hear what we are saying. By establishing eye contact, asking open-ended questions, clarifying, validating, mirroring, summarizing, reframing, acknowledging, and using similar communication techniques, we can learn more about what made the other person angry, and at the same time sidestep escalation by not responding in kind or running away, but by trying to find the source of the anger.

2. **Invite your opponent's honest response.** Withhold your immediate response, realize that angry people need to vent their emotions, and do not take what they say personally. Understand that they are angry about what you *did.* If your adversary does not approve of who you *are,* he or she probably has not separated who you are from what you do, and in any event, everyone is entitled to their opinion, which should not make the least difference to you. It is usually our own fragility that makes us angry and defensive. The largest part of anger has little to do with the people we direct it against but correctly targets their actions; anger at others often is only self-anger that we have redirected toward a convenient external target.

3. **Ask for what you want.** Seeing conflict as an opportunity starts by indicating clearly, honestly, and without rancor your own needs and self-interests. Giving in to anger only encourages the conflict, reduces the possibility of victory on both sides, and allows the other person to doubt your integrity and trustworthiness. Asking for what we want and need is essential to converting an expression of anger into a bilateral statement of needs and desires so that a negotiation can take place between equals.

4. **Clearly state the problem.** This seems easier than it actually is, since the presenting problem may not express the underlying reasons for its existence or continuation. As long as the focus is on gaining the other person's attention or saying what we want or need, no dialogue is possible. To have a dialogue, we need a single

agreed-upon point of reference, which may be a neutralized or impartial statement of what the conflict is actually about.

5. **Brainstorm alternatives.** List all the alternative ways the problem might be solved. Most people like to believe that a problem can have only one solution, which is their position or how they would like to resolve it. Jointly identifying alternative solutions helps shift the focus away from the problem and toward the solution.

6. **Focus on interests rather than positions.** Conflict becomes an opportunity when the dialogue shifts from *positions* (what we want) to *interests* (why we want it). Interests are rarely mutually exclusive and can be satisfied in multiple ways, whereas positions are nearly always in opposition and represent only one of many possible outcomes. Positions are cognitive traps that narrow thinking, perception, and the range of possible outcomes. Interests broaden these and focus on the future rather than the past. This step will be easier to take if you can be clear about your own interests and willing to listen to your opponents interests. Generosity by one side is often matched by a responsive generosity on the other side, just as anger is often responded to by a matching anger.

7. **Look for criteria.** Criteria are standards, or rules for resolving the dispute fairly. Criteria allow anger to shift in the direction of problem solving and can help the parties focus on how to make their agreements work in practice.

8. **Separate what works from what doesn't.** We have found many ways of separating the approaches that are capable of resolving the dispute from those that only result in frustration. Roger Fisher and Bill Ury write about some of these in their excellent book on negotiation, *Getting to Yes.* Here are some of the "separations" that work:
   - Separate people from problems.
   - Separate personalities from behavior.
   - Separate empathy from judgment.
   - Separate listening from problem solving.
   - Separate process from content.
   - Separate positions from interests.
   - Separate problems from solutions.

- Separate emotions from analysis.
- Separate analysis from negotiation.
- Separate the future from the past.
- Separate options from choices.
- Separate criteria from selection.
- Separate agreements from differences.
- Separate yourself from others.
- Separate acknowledgment from feedback.
- Separate feedback from evaluation.
- Separate ending from closure.

Coaching to Reveal the Opportunities in Conflict

In one of our more difficult assignments, we were called in to work with a department that was being torn apart by conflict. Barbara, an innovative manager with very poor people skills, was trying to transform the organization from top to bottom. Rick, the leader of a very strong union, was locked in a personality and power conflict with Barbara. Everyone in the department had chosen sides and had an opinion about the problem. We tried everything, from large group meetings where we tried to build a community of common goals for the coming year to one-on-one mediated sessions.

Barbara did not seem to be able to help herself. She continually undid the progress we made with a clumsy remark or undermining behavior. The result was that Rick would fly into a rage and escalate the conflict. Finally, we realized that the only way to resolve the conflict was by helping Barbara adopt new behaviors that would not trigger angry responses from Rick, and by helping Rick to respond more calmly. We hoped our strategy would also win the rest of the organization's support for the changes Barbara advocated, and would motivate Rick to change as well.

We gave the following coaching to Barbara to support her in coming up with strategies she could use to transform the conflict into an opportunity for growth. We think they apply not just to her, but to many other managers who find themselves locked in conflict with their peers and subordinates. As you read these coaching strategies, consider whether they might apply to you or to other people in your organization.

1. **The conflict is not about "them" or what "they" do, but about how you handle it.** It is easy to slip into criticizing what others do, but doing so lets you off the hook and fails to recognize that you can improve the way you handle them. Ignore their behavior and focus only on the success or failure of your responses.

2. **Don't say, "We tried that and it didn't work." Say, "How can we do it so it will work?"** The fact that earlier efforts failed means nothing. Perhaps they failed because the timing or mood wasn't right, because the intention was untrusting or suspicious, because there wasn't a 100 percent commitment, because the underlying problems hadn't surfaced, or because the process was flawed. Don't ask if what the other person said is right or true, but what is right or true about it; not what went wrong, but what can I learn from what happened.

3. **It doesn't matter what you meant. What matters is what they hear and they don't hear your meaning.** If they don't think that they have been heard, you haven't been listening well enough. The next time you hear a criticism, do not respond defensively, but with a clarifying question, such as, What did I do that caused you to feel that way? or Can you tell me more? or What can I do to solve that problem?

4. **The conflict is not about you; it's about the problem.** You are not the problem, and neither are they. The problem is an "it," not a "you" or a "them." When you personalize a problem, it becomes emotional and concerned with rejection and loyalty. When you de-personalize a problem, it becomes an obstacle that can be overcome by a good strategy.

5. **You don't own the solution.** You don't have to make it happen. If you own the solution, by definition you also own the problem. If what you want is collaboration, you have to *not* fix it yourself. If every time a child is asked to do the dishes, a parent steps in and does them instead, the child never learns how to take responsibility for washing them. And yes, the dishes in the beginning may not be as clean as you would like them to be.

6. **Ignore the content, watch the process.** We are easily hypnotized by the problem and lose sight of the solution. Ignore the problem and

focus on creating a problem-solving process that has the capacity to improve the way you respond and the way others respond to you.

7. **Invite criticism.** Go out of your way to seek out those you disagree with and ask them what you can do to improve your skills. After every conversation, ask for feedback about how you did and what you might do better. Take notes and work on improving your responses.

8. **Everything that really matters is relationships and interaction.** Relationships make a group into a team, a house into a home. If you push too hard for what you want, you may get it and lose what really matters. If you focus on building relationships, you will eventually get what you want.

9. **Drop the victim role. Play the hero.** Don't slip into feeling sorry for yourself. If you buy the victim behavior, others will too, and you will lose the power of selfless action. Do not talk about what anyone has done to you. Talk only about what you plan to do. Drop the past completely and speak only of the present and the future.

10. **The conflict is not about fault, it's about an opportunity for improvement.** Begin with the assumption that you brought the conflict on yourself, that you *chose* every one of the results you now see. Then let it all go, because blaming doesn't help unless you want to get stuck. Leadership is not about fault or even about taking responsibility, but about creating a sense of collective responsibility that is beyond fault.

Coaching Notes for My Own Responses to Conflict: An Exercise

Which elements in our coaching of Barbara would you give to yourself? Consider your own process skills and the times you slip back into the old patterns of the reptile brain. In the following space, create a dialogue with yourself and list the points you would like to make in coaching yourself to create a more healthy and effective approach to conflict. Check your ideas with people you know for their feedback. If you are working with a partner, you might coach each other. If you are working with a team, compare the coaching notes each of you has written. If you have much overlap, an underlying organizational or cultural pattern may be at play in the way you deal with conflict. You may then be able to combine forces to change that pattern.

1. _____
2. _____
3. _____
4. _____
5. _____

Opportunities that Are Implicit in Conflict

Conflict creates many opportunities for increased communication, learning, growth, change, improved relationships, and deeper understanding. These opportunities are maximized when we shift our conflict paradigms from ones that demonize the "other," that victimize or justify the "self," that distort the subject of the dispute, that limit what is possible in these relationships, or that keep us from learning from the dispute. We find these opportunities are implicit in the conflict once we begin to approach it collaboratively. As you review the following conflict lessons, reflect on what you have learned in each category from the conflicts in your own life and note them in the space provided.

1. **The other.** Conflict allows us to deepen the degree of empathy and intimacy we are able to experience with someone who disagrees with us. This lesson is often the case in families, but it is also true in the workplace, with neighbors, and inside organizations. Unresolved anger collapses the other person into a stereotyped villain, while dialogue in the midst of conflict resurrects the human side of his or her personality, allowing us to behave more humanely.

   _____
   _____
   _____

2. **The self.** Conflict allows for growth, realization, and self-improvement, which anger and shame diminish. Through conflict we may recognize that our behavior has not had the effect we

intended it to have or that we need to take greater responsibility for our lives or that we are more capable of speaking clearly to our opponents than we think. As a result, we feel empowered when we overcome our conflicts and weakened when we run from them or fight back.

_____

_____

_____

3. **The subject of the dispute.** Conflict is an opportunity to learn more about what doesn't work in order to be able to fix it. Solutions depend on problems, which depend on communication, which depends on halting the escalation so as to be able to see the opportunity that exists within the conflict and thus improve what isn't working. Different, even opposing points of view, help create a larger and more varied picture of the problem, which leads to richer, more comprehensive, and effective solutions.

_____

_____

_____

4. **The relationship.** Having gained some understanding of the other, the self and the problem, the interaction between them needs to be considered. A manager and an employee may have a conflict over what work needs to be done, but the reason the conflict escalates may have more to do with the history and quality of their relationship and the way they have communicated their needs and unspoken expectations to each other than with anything else. Conflicts are opportunities to improve our relationships, which helps prevent future conflicts.

_____

_____

_____

5. **The nature of conflict.** Awareness of process, of how we get angry, of why, and of whom we have chosen to engage with in conflict, allows us to reach a deeper level of understanding of the conflicts we experience repeatedly or chronically, and to be less inclined to blame others for our own lack of skill in communication. Conflict is the "opportunity of opportunities," that allows us to gain insight into our feelings and actions and those of others, so we can prevent our conflicts from escalating to the point where these opportunities become hidden.

   If we can learn to look at conflict as a challenge rather than a burden, as something positive, as concealing an enormous potential for growth and change, we may begin to anticipate with pleasure the next chance we get to turn our conflicts into exercises in skill building and opportunities for positive change. As we approach our conflicts with a new spirit, we may also start to see whole new levels of the conflict to analyze and work on, and deeper levels of resolution become possible.

   Often, as we are mediating a conflict, its complexion, focus and nature will start to change dramatically. In a recent sexual harassment dispute we mediated, Sally claimed she had been the victim of unwanted touching when her boss, Fred, refused to stop grabbing her, massaging her shoulders, and trying to kiss her. Fred argued he had done nothing of the sort and was in fact totally uninterested in her sexually or in any way other than as an employee.

   As we probed deeper into their relationship, we found they had a long history of friendship that had taken place many years prior to working together. Sally expected to be promoted to the position Fred now occupied, and believed she had been passed over because she was a woman. Fred had made romantic advances to Sally many years ago but abandoned her to marry his current wife.

   As the mediation unfolded and the pain of many years emerged for Sally, the conflict took on a different cast. Their understanding of the nature of their relationship deepened, and the resolution they created was not based on sexual harassment, but on putting their disappointed hopes and dreams to rest.

Identifying the Conflicts in Your Organization: An Exercise

Now that we have described the opportunities that can come from constructively engaging our conflicts and resolving them, you may want to return to the conflicts you identified in the early pages of this chapter. The next questionnaire asks you to go beneath the surface of a conflict you are presently having, or have experienced in the past year, and to analyze the incident by answering a number of questions about it. Notice if your understanding of the conflict evolves and becomes richer as you explore the answers to these questions. See if you can identify ways you might be able to resolve these issues or turn them into opportunities for growth and learning.

1. Identify one incident that occurred during the past year in your organization that you wish had been handled differently.

    _____

    _____

    _____

2. Name two to four individuals who would need to talk to each other in order to resolve the incident fully or handle it differently in the future.

    _____

    _____

    _____

3. What conflict styles are these individuals presently using to respond to the conflict?

    _____

    _____

    _____

4. Are these conflict styles effective in resolving the conflict? If not, why not?

_____

_____

_____

5. Indicate one thing that will happen if this dispute is not resolved.

_____

_____

_____

6. What opportunities for personal change, organizational growth, or learning are presented for both sides by this conflict?

_____

_____

_____

7. What steps could be taken to help resolve it?

_____

_____

_____

8. Write down one thing you would be willing to do to help resolve it.

_____

_____

_____

9. What is one thing you need to do to let go of the conflict yourself?

_____

_____

_____

10.   How has your understanding of the conflict evolved or changed as you answered these questions? How would it change if you actually did the things you identified above?

_____

_____

_____

Resolving Disputes by Consensus

Organizational disputes are often generated by the false expectations that surround the decision making process. The five basic ways of making organizational decisions follow.

Notification:	"The following decision has been made and will be implemented."
Consultation:	"I would like your thoughts on this issue before I make a decision."
Voting:	"Let the majority decide."
Consensus:	"I am willing to abide by the consensus of the group if the decision meets my needs and interests."
Unanimity:	"We must reach complete agreement in order to implement this solution."

Consensus is a collaborative group process for making decisions everyone can support. Its purpose is to allow people in organizations to choose among several options, ensure that everyone has an equal voice, promote understanding and ownership, allow differences of opinion to surface, build unity and a sense of common direction, encourage collaborative thinking, and prevent sabotage after the decision is made. Consensus is not the same as unanimity and does not mean coerced approval. It is an acceptance of the wisdom of the group.

Most conflicts occur because consensus is not used, or because managers sound as if they are creating a consensus process, but really want only to consult with others on the decisions they are going to make themselves. Conflicts also take place when consensus fails to result in a decision. If you are in an organization that is unable to reach consensus, here are some of the things that you can still do.

♦   Separate the issues over which there is no consensus to return to later.

- Agree not to make a decision.
- Table the decision until later.
- Bring in an outside expert to advise the group.
- Return to vision or goals; then develop procedures or guidelines that flow from them.
- Break the issues down into separate parts and try to reach consensus on each part separately. Look for hidden issues.
- Use group brainstorming to invent options.
- Separate into factions and ask each group to meet separately and list five suggestions for compromise.
- Create a team composed of representatives from each side to prioritize options and recommend solutions.
- Look at each of the objections to see if solutions can be created to those, while moving ahead with the proposal.
- Take a break or return the decision to the group for additional problem solving.
- Refer the issue to a completely uninvolved group to develop compromise solutions.
- Bring in an outside facilitator to help bring about consensus.
- Bring in an outside mediator to help resolve the dispute.
- Vote based on majority rule.
- Prepare majority and minority reports.
- Allow the minority group to continue to convince others to change their minds.
- Allow the group's primary decision maker to decide the issue.

Mediation: The Path to Resolving Workplace Disputes

The most effective all-round method for resolving difficult interpersonal and organizational disputes is mediation, in which a neutral third party helps those involved discuss their problems, communicate with one another, and negotiate mutually agreeable, voluntary solutions. Many organizations are now using mediation to resolve conflicts before they escalate into lawsuits or grievances. Some of our clients, especially those with major change efforts underway, are creating internal mediation teams in their human resources departments or are using outside mediators such as ourselves to resolve their disputes. Others are hiring ombudsmen to act as neutrals and investigate or mediate disputes. Training employees to function as peer mediators is another important resource for organizational conflict resolution.

Mediation often succeeds because it encourages each party to listen and understand the other party's position, promotes open and honest communication, minimizes personality conflicts, structures interactions to prevent the escalation of interpersonal conflict, reduces stress, and encourages mutual problem solving. It allows feelings to surface, validates concerns, promotes individual responsibility for conflict, and encourages cooperation, healing, and partnership. It succeeds in about 90 percent of the cases, with fewer enforcement problems because agreements are reached voluntarily.

Mediation encourages employees and managers to recognize their destructive patterns and identify the group processes that lead to their conflicts. Here are two observations that resulted from an organizational mediation, in which we asked how people in the group thought the conflict had gotten to that stage of escalation in the first place:

Often there is a pattern of triangulation in which we talk about someone to a third person and do not take it to the person themselves. We put them down, we gossip about them, and we stir up scapegoating against each other. We should practice a policy that if you have a concern, you take it directly to the person involved.

There is a subtle element of one-up/one-down that is unsettling. It seems that someone has to be in the down seat. Discussions don't go deep enough because no one wants to be in the down seat. If you have bad news that you have to give, you are the odd person out, and it is hard get to clarity on what you need because the discussion is veiled. This results in everyone being fearful of being honest and hiding their true feelings from the group.

In the mediation process, the parties do not perceive each other as "inhuman supervisors" or as "arrogant, trouble-making employees." Rather, they are taken out of their stereotypes and encouraged to communicate on a direct, personal, and human level. Responsibility for communication and results is not placed on someone else, but on the parties themselves.

Mediation is confidential and future oriented, as opposed to legal procedures that are public and focused on the past. Mediation is less concerned with deciding who was right or wrong than with straightening out the problem so it does not occur again. In mediation, the focus is on finding practical solutions, and on surfacing and letting go of emotional issues that need to be ventilated, even when they cannot be resolved. Often what people in conflict want most is for someone simply to listen.

Mediation can also help resolve the interpersonal conflicts that occur in every workplace—the petty dislikes and jealousies, the personality conflicts and problems in communication, the long-standing hostilities and conflicting interests, the competition and perceived favoritism. These conflicts disrupt work and interfere with productivity, yet they are left to smolder, forcing employees to suffer in silent rage or to express their frustration and anger in counterproductive ways, such as through illness, resignation, disruption, resistance to change, violence, retribution, strikes, or slowdowns.

In any workplace, it is better to bring these tensions to the surface and allow the opponents to explore alternative ways of thinking and acting which avoid disruptive results, than it is to ignore even petty interpersonal problems and assume they will go away or force solutions from above. The following examples of workplace mediations we have performed illustrate some of the advantages of mediation, including its ability to promote organizational learning.

In one case, representatives for the company and the union thought mediation would be a waste of time, since the union was insisting that a fired employee be reinstated, while the company insisted on her termination. Instead of canceling the mediation, we met privately with each side and asked the company representatives to list all the reasons they did not want the grievant to work for them.

We then asked them to think of their reasons as *conditions* for reinstatement, since if the employee were able to prove to the company's satisfaction that she could meet every one of their conditions, there would be no reason left for not reinstating her. Over several hours of mediation, the parties developed a set of conditions for the employee's return that were satisfactory to the company, the union, and the employee, including an agreement that the employee would maintain perfect attendance for a period of three months. Because the employee wanted to build trust and demonstrate that she was committed to the agreement, she voluntarily agreed to increase the period to six months! The company was impressed, and each party felt vindicated by the result, since an arbitrator might have ruled either way if forced to decide on a long-term employee's discharge.

In a second mediation, an employee was also terminated for absenteeism, allegedly as a result of drug use, and the company was again determined not to reinstate him, but was prepared to make a token "nuisance" payment to avoid arbitration. The grievant had found a new job and did not really want reinstatement, but the union was determined to press the issue because it thought the employee had not received due process, and abandoning the case seemed like a condonation of the company's abuse of employee rights.

The parties were asked to brainstorm ideas for how to prevent similar drug cases from occurring in the future. In an off-the-record discussion, they came up with a number of creative preventative techniques, and designed a settlement that included a token payment to the grievant, a company agreement to use better procedures in the future, and a commitment to fund a joint training program that would help union stewards and line managers identify and handle issues of employee drug abuse.

In another mediation, a sales associate for a large manufacturing company received a negative evaluation and decided to resign. A few days later she had second thoughts and asked her supervisor if she could revoke her letter of resignation. When the supervisor checked with her human relations manager, she was told she had the option of accepting the resignation, which the supervisor decided to do. The union protested saying the company had not accepted the resignation before the employee had retracted it, and both sides came to mediation to do battle over whether the employee had a legal right to withdraw her resignation.

Instead, the parties were encouraged to talk about the underlying issues: What did the company think was wrong with the employee's performance? What were the reasons that led her to resign? Why had she changed her mind? Why did the company not want to let her withdraw her resignation? A number of false perceptions and problems of communication surfaced, including indications that the employee had engaged in fraud. The employee did not enjoy doing sales work, yet an arbitrator might have put her back to work because the evidence was unclear. Instead, both sides agreed on a set of rules for how to handle resignations in the future, the employee voluntarily left the company, and the possible fraud was never placed in her record because her resignation was left in place.

A simple mediation process that can be used by employees or managers to resolve a large number of workplace disputes includes the following steps:

1. **Introduction to the Process.** The employee or manager as mediator welcomes the parties, asks everyone to introduce themselves, and establishes the ground rules for the mediation.
2. **Storytelling.** Each party explains the conflict from his or her point of view. The employee or manager uses active listening skills to clarify, restate, and summarize; asks questions that will help both parties understand the problems better; acknowledges and validates important issues and feelings; and identifies issues for negotiation.
3. **Problem Solving and Negotiation.** The employee or manager helps the disputants to negotiate collaboratively to reach a fair solution by encouraging both parties to focus on problems rather than people; on interests, rather than positions; on the future, rather than the past; on generating options to solve the problem; on finding mutually satisfactory solutions; on prioritizing them; and on looking for resolutions that could prevent the same type of conflict from occurring in the future.
4. **Agreement.** Agreements are written down in an informal contract, which is very specific in terms of who will do what, when, where, and so on. The agreement is balanced and nonjudgmental, and signed, with copies given to both parties.
5. **Closure.** Once agreement has been reached, the employee or manager compliments the parties on their successes and on the lessons learned, confirms their ownership of the agreement, and sends them away feeling good about themselves and what they have accomplished.

How Organizations Handle Conflict

In many public and private sector organizations, efforts by executives or managers to resolve work-related conflicts are viewed with suspicion, primarily owing to the perception, and in many cases the reality, of *significant* conflicts of interest on the part of the people who are trying to resolve them. In many of these organizations, human resource (HR) personnel or mid-level managers are assigned the task of trying to resolve disputes, but are given little training, and are often viewed as a kind of

Praetorian guard, whose primary role is not so much to solve the problem as to protect the organization, even if it results in a failure to redress legitimate complaints.

While employees often resist the resolution of their complaints because they feel these conflict resolvers only represent the interests of management, supervisors and managers feel they are biased toward employees, that they are too "touchy feely," and that they are not interested in managerial issues such as performance, profitability, or efficiency.

In truth, HR departments and in-house managerial mediators do have a conflict of interest, as they are often required by the organizations they work for to simultaneously represent employees, managers, and the organization, leading to a loss of trust by all involved. Their dual role perpetuates an organizational culture that permits double messages, secrecy, manipulations, half-truths, and officialese, as opposed to promoting honesty, openness, empathy, negotiation, and collaborative problem solving. Tremendous stress is placed on the in-house conflict resolvers who are required to respond in these contradictory ways, leading to personal stress, confusion, moral equivocation, loss of judgment, inflexibility, and a kind of "role schizophrenia" based on the "double bind" messages they have been given. If these employees, managers, or conflict resolvers wish to advance their own careers within the organization, it may be wise for them to pay greater attention to the needs and wishes of upper management than to those of lower-level employees who have fewer career advancing capabilities.

Finally, if the purpose of organizational mediation is not merely to settle, smooth over, or get rid of the conflict, but also to actually resolve it, to use it as an opportunity for growth and change, to learn from it as an organization, and to generate healing and rebuild trust in the workforce, someone needs to be available to intervene and work with the conflict without being perceived as having a bias or power-based perspective that could limit the organization's ability to accomplish these goals. If the conflict resolver is a party to the dispute, is politically in favor of one of the parties, or has a partial responsibility for outcomes, these results will be nearly impossible to achieve.

The problem, then, is to design a multidimensional system for resolving workplace disputes that works on a variety of different levels, uses resources from inside and outside the organization, permits employees and managers to feel heard, and transforms the conflict into an opportunity for organizational learning.

Problems with Organizational Neutrality

If we are going to make collaborative, low-cost conflict resolution alternatives effective and increase resolution and organizational learning, disputing parties need to be able to trust the process. For employees and managers to arrive at an effective level of trust in the workplace while they are in the midst of conflict is difficult under the best of circumstances. To succeed, they need to have a clear and unambiguous answer by organizational conflict resolvers to the question: *Which side are you on?*

In most cases, in-house conflict resolvers cannot answer this question without considerable hedging, ambiguity, and doubt. The approach most organizational conflict resolvers have taken has been to identify themselves as "neutrals" in the dispute, but this claim has several difficulties.

1. **Complete neutrality does not exist.** Everyone in an organization has had experiences that shift their perceptions, attitudes, and expectations. Managers and HR representatives have a point of view because they work for the organization that is being disrupted by the conflict.

2. **All conflicts generate distrust and polarization,** so it is difficult for anyone in conflict to believe other people can be neutral. Neutrality is seen as a mask for partiality or indifference. Conflicting employees and organizations are concerned with both the actuality and the appearance of neutrality.

3. **Neutrality requires emotional distancing** from both parties and does not encourage emotional honesty, intimate communication, self-criticism, shared responsibility, a search for prevention and proactive solutions, organizational learning, or healing. Objectivity often means suppressing subjectivity. But subjectivity is important to conflict resolvers as a gateway to empathy. To employees, the most important aspect of neutrality is not perspective, objectivity, or judgment, but honesty and a lack of bias.

4. **Neutrality is a straitjacket.** It does not encourage the parties in a conflict to openly express their feelings or to acknowledge their grief, compassion, love, anger, fear, shame, or hope, any of which

may need to be released during the process in order to resolve the underlying reasons for the dispute.

5. **When confronted with a paradox, contradiction, or enigma, neutrality will be incapable of resolving it** without ignoring or eliminating the very duality that feeds it, and organizations are riddled with dualities, paradoxes, contradictions, and enigmas.

True neutrality cannot exist without partiality or advocacy. Advocates who offer articulate reasons on behalf of each side can facilitate the finding of neutral ground. Neutrality only exists against a backdrop of partiality. What is required, then, is less organizational *neutrality*, than a lack of organizational *bias*, which expresses itself in the ability of the dispute resolver to be *on both parties' sides at the same time*, to advocate for the employee, the manager, the organization, and the dispute-resolution process simultaneously. But how is it possible to be an advocate and unbiased at the same time?

The Uses and Misuses of Advocacy

Advocacy is usually seen as a hindrance to the dispute resolution process, often because of a strong desire among conflict resolvers in organizations for the dispute simply to go away, as opposed to taking the time and energy to work through it, resolve it, learn from it, and genuinely accept it as an opportunity for transformation, team building, learning, and growth. But advocacy is also seen as a hindrance because third parties who advocate or present the ideas of others often do so in ways that discourage compromise and collaboration.

Encouraging advocacy appears counterintuitive to dispute resolvers because it increases polarization, drives the parties further apart, substitutes debate for dialogue, encourages posturing rather than listening, and hardens positions rather than softening them. The ideas we have about third-party advocacy are drawn primarily from our negative experiences with attorneys, whose adversarial behavior often makes it more difficult to settle a dispute.

On the other hand, at its best, advocacy is simply a technique for clarifying genuine points of difference. It is capable of improving the quality of dialogue by making certain that opposing ideas, rather than the people who champion them, do battle. At its worst, advocacy is sophism, in which the search is not for truth or agreement, but victory, often by means of secrecy, illusion, and trickery.

Advocacy is at its best when the ground rules are clear and when a mediator or facilitator is present whose purpose is to hold the common ground; to draw the advocates and the parties into a circle; to clarify communication; to encourage responsiveness and reduce defensiveness; to draw rhetoric away from rationalization, demonization, and victimization, and toward the truth. It is also at its best when it does not distort or minimize what actually happened in the name of "presenting a better case," but seeks to reach agreement and integrate perspectives on what actually happened.

Third-party advocacy in organizations is a way of giving voice to employees who have been silenced or intimidated, or are unstable or inarticulate, but whose ideas are still worth considering. It is a way of expressing the best possible reasons in support of all the alternative ways of resolving a dispute so that there is a better chance of choosing correctly, and of allowing everyone involved to feel that they have been fully and deeply heard.

Many organizations encourage employees or managers who have disputes to pick someone from within the workplace to be their advocate before an internal review board. Peers often make better advocates than professionals because they understand the workplace better. Using peer advocates instead of professionals also reduces the cost of the proceedings.

While professional advocates are trained to argue both sides of a question, peer advocates are more often motivated to find the truth, and are willing to be convinced by the other side. In cases where a manager or employee is found to be lying, a peer advocate who continues to work in the organization will suffer a loss of reputation for having advocated on behalf of a person who did not tell the truth.

Advocacy is useful in the search for truth because it is a way of perfecting the logic of opposition, of finding the hidden truths that are contained in opposites—and in the things that unite them, in what they have in common. Truth without unity is adversarial and divisive, while truth without opposition is simplistic and static. Opposition is the generative source of freedom, growth, change, and independence, while unity stimulates responsibility, community, continuity, and connection. People and organizations cannot learn or improve without both.

The reason advocacy so often obscures the truth is that opposition is allowed to prevail over unity of purpose. Winning becomes more important than learning, and the adversarial nature of the advocacy process permits a shortsightedness that tends to obscure its long-range collaborative intent. To avoid the false character of one-sided self-interest, we need to create a systemic design in which the parts are counterbalanced to express the interests of the whole.

Peer advocacy, by allowing employees who are not professionals to help others prepare and present the reasons supporting their requests, assists the organization in hearing issues more objectively and reaching fair decisions, without doing so on the basis of past history, personality, or position in the organization.

Advocacy as it is used in the law rarely results in truth or justice, and then only because each side is taken with a grain of salt. This failure of the law is partly because the loyalty of the advocate is to the narrow and immediate self-interest of the client. Legal advocacy is incapable of recognizing or acknowledging the legitimacy of any claim or interest other than the one retaining it. No organization can withstand that kind of advocacy. But peer advocates are not encouraged to disregard the interest of the organization or of any of the people working inside it, and can help employees and managers feel they are being treated fairly.

Using Advocacy to Encourage Dialogue Rather than Debate

If we think of advocates not as hired guns, but as protectors of fairness, as searchers after truth, and as mediators or resolvers of conflict, the polarizing debates that occur in all conflicts prevent them and the organization from achieving these goals. To promote fairness, learning and resolution we need to transform *debate* into *dialogue.*

Physicist David Bohm defined dialogue as "a stream of meaning flowing among, through and between us." Dialogue is a form of thinking together, or "participatory consciousness," in which thought behaves almost like an organism, drawing its disparate parts into a whole. Dialogue helps create a sense of community, group learning, and trust, and is the way many conflicts get resolved. The following outline clarifies the differences between dialogue and debate.

Dialogue	Debate
1. Dialogue is collaborative: two or more sides work together toward a common understanding.	Debate is oppositional: two sides are opposed and attempt to prove each other wrong.
2. In dialogue, finding common ground is the goal.	In debate, the goal is to win.
3. In dialogue, one listens in order to find commonalities.	In debate, one listens in order to find flaws and counter arguments.
4. Dialogue enlarges and possibly alters a participant's point of view.	Debate affirms a participant's own point of view.
5. Dialogue reveals assumptions for reevaluation.	Debate defends assumptions as truth.
6. Dialogue encourages introspection into one's own position.	Debate rarely results in introspection.
7. Dialogue opens the possibility of reaching a better solution than any of the original solutions.	Debate defends one's own positions as the best solution and excludes other solutions.
8. Dialogue creates open minds, an openness to being wrong and to change.	Debate creates closed minds, a focus on being right and resisting change.
9. Dialogue calls for temporarily suspending one's beliefs.	Debate calls for investing completely in one's beliefs.
10. In dialogue, one searches for basic agreements.	In debate, one searches for glaring difficulties.
11. In dialogue, one searches for strengths in the other positions.	In debate, one searches for flaws and weaknesses in the other positions.
12. Dialogue involves a real concern for the other person and seeks not to alienate or offend.	Debate involves opposing the other position without focusing on feelings or relationships and belittles or deprecates the person.
13. Dialogue assumes that there are many right answers, that many people have pieces of it, and that together they can create a workable solution.	Debate assumes that there is a single right answer and that one side has it.
14. Dialogue is open ended.	Debate implies a conclusion.
15. Dialogue assumes that conflict is resolvable.	Debate assumes that conflict is only resolvable when one side wins.

(Sources: David Bohm, Shelley Berman, and the Dialogue Group of the Boston Chapter of Educators for Social Responsibility)

How do you stimulate dialogue when you find yourself in the middle of a debate? How do you advocate so as to encourage dialogue, as opposed to debate? One method is not to focus on making arguments, but on asking questions that require an answer that forces the parties to shift their thinking to a different context or paradigm regarding the conflict. The following questions can be used by advocates, as well as by conflicting parties, mediators, facilitators, and other organizational conflict resolvers, to shift adversarial group, interpersonal, and organizational debate in the direction of dialogue:

- What do you want? Why do you want it? What does the other person want? Why do they want it?
- What life experiences have led you to believe or think that? What has led you to feel so passionately about it? Why do you think that?
- What parts of your position do you have doubts about or not entirely agree with? What areas might create problems?
- What are the gray areas, the issues you find difficult to define precisely?
- Would you try to state the other person's position? Was their statement of your position accurate? Why has the other person taken that position? What are the arguments in favor of it? Are these reasonable or accurate?
- What do you see as your common interests, goals, and values? At some level, do you both want the same things?
- Can you agree on a joint statement of your differences?
- Do your differences reveal any riddles, paradoxes, contradictions, or enigmas?
- Is it possible to see your differences as polarities, as two sides of the same coin? What is the part that unites you? What is the coin?
- What would happen if you won completely and the other side lost or disappeared? Would you have lost anything? What would you have lost?
- Can you separate the issues you disagree over from the person you are disagreeing with?
- What process rules would help you disagree more constructively?
- Instead of focusing on the past, what would you like to see happen in the future?
- Are you disagreeing over fundamental values or over how to achieve them?
- Is it possible for both of you to be right or for an outsider to agree with both of these ideas or propositions? How?

- Would it be possible to test out these ideas in practice and see which one works best? How could we do that?
- What criteria should we look at to decide which idea works best?
- If we have to chose between alternatives, what can we do to improve each alternative? Can some of the ideas contained in the other person's position be incorporated into yours?
- What will be lost by choosing between these alternatives? Is there any other alternative?
- Can this dialogue be ongoing? Can we preserve these different perspectives so we do not lose sight of their unique truths? How?
- What do you think should be done to improve the process for handling conflicts or disagreements in the future?

Another way advocates can use these questions to move debate in the direction of dialogue is to consider them as roles that can be played by anyone in the conflict, whether they are the advocate, the mediator, the managerial dispute resolver, or the parties. For example, the following chart presents a number of dialogue-encouraging roles, along with a question or comment that illustrates how each might help shift the conflict resolution process in the direction of dialogue:

Role	Question or Comment
Inquiring:	"What do you think should be done? Why do you think so?"
Supporting:	"Here's an idea that supports your point."
Acknowledging:	"You took a risk in making that point."
Refereeing:	"What ground rules do we need so everyone can feel that the process has been fair?"
Concretizing:	"Can you give me an example or analogy?"
Exploring:	"Tell me more about why you feel so strongly about this issue."
Summarizing:	"Is this what you are trying to say. . .?"
Challenging:	"Isn't that inconsistent with what you said before?"
Coaching:	"Could you find a way to respond less personally?"
Connecting:	"That point connects directly with what A said earlier."
Summarizing:	"Tell me if this is what you mean. . ."
Reorienting:	"I think we're lost. Can we get back on track?" "Are we talking about the real issue?"
Problem solving:	"What are some possible solutions?"
Uniting:	"Why have we come together to discuss this issue? What do we have in common?"
Mediating:	"What would it take to resolve our differences?"

Conflict Resolution Systems Design

Conflict resolution systems design is an analytical tool that allows organizations to respond strategically to chronic conflicts and is based on a set of concepts developed by William Ury, Stephen Goldberg, and Jeanne Brett in *Getting Disputes Resolved*. Systems can be planned to discourage dysfunctional behaviors so that teams do not get into conflicts based on their old patterns, but use collaborative processes to create healthier interactions. The following interviews with employees from very different kinds of organizations indicate some relatively easy ways systems can be implemented to prevent chronic tensions, poor communication, and unwanted conflicts:

We should have better communication between departments. I hate the memo wars.

We should sit down and come up with solutions face-to-face. We have to be more open with each other and share information. Information is power and we should be giving it to each other.

We need to have an agenda for our meetings and be more inclusive of everyone so we can argue out the issues. But to do this there needs to be more structure to our meetings.

We have the most unproductive meetings of anyplace I have ever been. The agenda is created at rather than before the meeting. We always start by introducing ourselves, and we do this over and over again. I have gotten to the point where I know what everyone is going to say before they say it.

Our process needs to be responsive to the needs of the institution. Budget and personnel issues have to be handled in a more structured way so people can know how to prepare for a meeting. If we could do that, we could report out more consistently and this would speed up our meetings. And we should create a schedule and a proposed agenda for the year with a month-by-month plan so we know what we are going to be discussing.

Once decisions are made, notes should be kept and a memo sent out saying this is now law. Everyone on the team should support it whether or not they voted for it. Put it in writing so if it affects other departments, they know what we did.

We need an established channel for the whole organization to get information and decisions in a timely way. It would be helpful to have departmentwide meetings with established agendas. We need to understand that we are customers for each other. We should try to break down rigid lines between departments. We need to respect and have mutual understanding of what others trying to do.

One of the organizational purposes of conflict resolution systems design is to shift the initial choices available to conflicting parties in trying to resolve their disputes from the use of power to the use of rights and interest-based alternatives, such as mediation and collaborative negotiation. For this reason, conflict resolution systems design methods argue for the creation of organizational structures and systems to resolve disputes based on the following principles:

1. **Focus on improving interest-based alternatives.** Most of the techniques used by organizations to resolve disputes are based either on power (the boss decides who is right) or rights (the employee files a complaint and a manager decides whether there was a violation of company policy). Mediation is an alternative based on interests (the employee and the manager meet together and agree what kind of relationship they want or need with each other, and talk about how to solve the problem) that organizations need to devote greater energies and resources to developing.

2. **Provide low-cost rights and power backups.** If mediation and other interest-based methods do not work, the organization will need to find a rights- or power-based system as backups to finally resolve the dispute, and should develop low-cost methods such as arbitration, which, are less costly than litigation.

3. **Arrange procedures from low to high cost.** Make sure the organization encourages employees to use mediation as a first step, rather than waiting until the dispute has caused irreparable damage or litigation has started.

4. **Build in loopbacks to negotiation.** If mediation or informal problem solving do not succeed at first, make sure employees can return to these forums later if other procedures do not resolve the dispute.

5. **Look for preventative measures.** Rather than wait for conflicts to blow up, the organization may want to put resources into preventing conflicts that are predictable, recurring, and chronic. Some useful techniques include consulting with complaining employees before the conflict gets out of hand; facilitating

informal communication and problem solving during the beginning phase of the conflict; and providing feedback, evaluation, and correction afterwards to make sure the problem is actually solved and does not reemerge in some other area.

6. **Build in motivation to use alternative procedures.** Organizations need to encourage their employees to use alternative conflict resolution procedures such as mediation and peer advocacy. Encouragement should include training in the skills and resources necessary to use them, and reward systems that motivate their use.

An Alternative Organizational Design

An alternative response to organizational conflict would be to preserve, promote and perfect the opposing truths of the conflict through a careful use of peer advocacy and dialogue, while simultaneously remembering and reinforcing the sense of organizational unity through mediation, and using the alternation between these contradictory forces to generate synergy, learning, and growth.

To do both at the same time requires a multifaceted approach to conflict resolution and an organizational system that combines advocacy on behalf of each of the parties with a variety of internal and external mediative structures, including a broad range of processes and roles that create opportunities for positive resolution and organizational learning.

In a dispute we recently mediated, four teachers at an intermediate public school were asked to meet with us to resolve a four-year-long dispute that had polarized the entire school. Two of the teachers were leaders of a local union that had been instrumental in firing a principal who had been supported by the other two teachers. The supporters had never understood why the principal had been fired, and the district refused to offer any reasons because confidential personnel issues were involved.

At the mediation, the critics were able to offer a number of informal yet convincing reasons why the principal had been fired, and the supporters were given an opportunity to criticize the way he had been terminated. The critics were asked to say one thing the principal had done well, and the supporters were asked to say one thing he had not done well. Once each side had advocated the other's position, both sides felt listened to and they were able to talk about the things they needed to do to make the school a better place to work. The teachers all agreed to speak at a strategic planning meeting that had been set for the following day, and to say one thing they had learned from the conflict. When the rest of the faculty heard their responses, consensus became possible and the change process began in earnest.

A range of alternatives spanning a variety of formal and informal techniques from low to high levels of intervention can be implemented by internal conflict resolvers, whether they are peer advocates, HR representatives, teams, co-workers, mid-level managers, or high-level supervisors. The following are the main organizational alternatives that should be included in the design of any organizational conflict resolution system, arranged in the probable order of their use:

1. Informal problem solving and off-the-record communication.
2. Training and skill building.
3. Peer counseling and mentoring.
4. Team discussion, intervention and confrontation.
5. Peer mediation and coaching.
6. Collaborative negotiation.
7. Ombuds investigation, and intervention.
8. Appeal, peer advocacy, and organizational review.
9. Outside professional mediation.
10. Final and binding arbitration.

How a Typical Workplace Conflict Might Be Resolved

To understand how these ideas might play out in practice, we would like to consider what they would look like from the perspective of the participants in a hypothetical dispute between an employee and a manager or supervisor.

Assuming a conflict over an employee's absenteeism in a large public or private sector organization, and a traditional HR group or a group of managers or employees in charge of conflict resolution, issues involving the employee's absenteeism might be handled as follows:

Informal Problem Solving and Off-the-Record Communication. Looking at the system from the point of view of the parties to the conflict, the first thing that would happen would be to try to solve the problem informally with the parties involved. On arrival at HR, the employee or supervisor would be encouraged to use informal methods to communicate directly with the person involved, and be trained or counseled on their communication and problem-solving skills, in an effort to eliminate disputes that can be resolved easily.

If the informal process does not result in resolution, the issue would be looked at carefully to decide on an appropriate starting point in the formal effort to resolve it. Perhaps the manager or employee needs additional training or skill building, or perhaps peer counseling or mentoring would solve the problem. If the dispute affects co-workers, it may require a team discussion, intervention, or confrontation. The team meeting might be assisted by a facilitator from outside if the dispute is potentially disruptive or involves more than one person on each side.

If these efforts are to no avail, peer mediation and coaching might be initiated, ideally with mediators who have been chosen by the parties. If entire teams are involved in the conflict, or people working in different departments, a collaborative negotiation process may result in a better solution. If these forums are unable to resolve the conflict, an ombuds office investigation or high-level intervention might uncover hidden issues, resulting in a change in policy or a fresh approach to conflict resolution.

An Approach to Peer Advocacy. Assuming the above efforts have been unsuccessful, peer advocates might be selected by each of the parties to help them flesh out the issues, to state them clearly without unnecessarily polarizing the other side, and to search for common ground. The process might begin with the selection of representatives to assist either or both of the parties as advocates or coaches. They would separately explain the conflict resolution process, investigate the facts, try to understand their parties' interests, marshal the evidence, prepare their best arguments, agree on ground rules for their dialogue, and encourage those they represent to listen and be open to *hearing* what the other side has to say.

To avoid the tendency of advocates to take over the dispute, disempower the parties, encourage their rationalization and defensiveness, and promote their own agendas, the advocates' roles should be clearly defined as ones of encouraging dialogue, rather than debate. The advocates might be trained and supported in being coaches to the parties and might not play a speaking role during hearings or joint sessions.

An internal peer-based co-mediation team might also be selected, perhaps by each party picking a mediator with the advice of a peer coach/advocate. The co-mediation team might not wait until the joint session, but could begin to independently investigate the issues and conduct private sessions with the parties or the coach/advocates in an effort to find a solution.

The parties could appoint or select an ombuds representative to be present as an observer for the purpose of drafting recommendations for improvement in organizational policy, procedures, structures, roles, and so on, and to summarize, from an organizational perspective, the lessons and proactive steps that need to be taken to prevent any future occurrence of this type of conflict.

Meeting Organizational Interests. The coach/advocates, mediators, and/or ombuds representative would follow the parties through the process, helping to distill the conflict, encouraging them privately to listen more to each other, supporting them in handling the stress created by the dispute, deepening their understanding of the conflict and what they may have personally contributed to it, and helping them to reach agreements, to let go of the conflict and begin to heal, to forgive each other, and to return to the workplace respecting each other.

Coordination and Training. Any of the roles we have mentioned can be played by anyone within the organization, even from inside the group or department that is struggling with the conflict. The central coordination of these roles, the training of people to fill them, and the continuous improvement of the dispute resolution process are organizational functions that need to be centralized so that policies and practices can be monitored and improved for the organization as a whole. Concentrating the mediation, coaching/advocacy, and ombuds roles inside the organization will encourage a high degree of training, skill building, organizational learning, and professionalism.

For a design such as the one outlined here to succeed, organizations would need to train employees to function as peer mediators, coach/advocates, and ombudsmen in areas such as communication, coaching and advocacy, problem solving, mediation, collaborative negotiation, and ways of increasing organizational learning. Managers and employees throughout the organization would need to understand the process, how to use the system, what to expect from it, and what they can do on their own to resolve disputes informally.

Some organizational issues will continue to require outside, professional mediation primarily because of the "politics" involved, the seriousness of the dispute, the complexity of the issues, the need for expertise, the presence of outside attorneys, the risks to the organization, the refusal of the parties to cooperate, the inability of the conflict resolvers to handle it, and similar reasons.

Yet the advantages to organizations of establishing a peer coaching/advocacy/mediation/ombuds system are numerous, and include the likelihood of a higher rate of resolution of employee disputes, greater participant satisfaction with the process, reduced likelihood of expensive litigation, and a far greater likelihood that something will be learned from the conflict, that the organization will be able to improve the way it functions, and that chronic conflicts will be prevented before they get out of hand and handled successfully when they do.

Even a slight reduction in the number of conflicts would produce an *enormous* savings in time, expense, energy, morale, and productivity, which make conflict far more costly than most organizations realize. More importantly, people will feel supported by the organization and the people they work with, and will be willing to do more in return.

The workplace is a community. Like all communities, it is strengthened and its diversity and capacity for teamwork are encouraged by the recognition that its members are able to respond more productively to conflict when they feel supported, encouraged, and listened to, than when they are silenced, discouraged, and blamed for it. The combination of peer advocacy, dialogue, and mediation helps create that environment.

The opportunities for learning and growth that become possible when we improve our conflict resolution skills, when we humanize the way we participate in disputes, when we listen and become more collaborative with each other, when we engage in dialogue and become coaches and advocates for our relationships with one another, these opportunities can transform our lives, both as individuals and as creators of the organizations in which we work.

EIGHT

Why Humanize the Way We Work?

Through a curious transposition peculiar to our times it is innocence that is called upon to justify itself.

ALBERT CAMUS

Camus was right. Autocratic, insensitive management, even the inhuman treatment of employees, are rarely required to justify themselves, while reasons are often demanded for why we should have more democracy, humanization, or empowerment in the workplace. The need for justification seems reversed.

Warren Bennis, one of the early proponents of democracy in the workplace, recently commented to us that he has been advocating many of the changes described in this book for more than 40 years, yet his proposals are only now starting to gain credibility and acceptance. Perhaps this delayed response is the result of trying to shift a deeply engrained paradigm which has been dominant for many years and is just now beginning to move.

The paradigm that still dominates most of our workplaces assumes that employees are incapable of responsibility; that they should not be given decision-making power; that they require explicit, detailed direction; and that they cannot perform the functions and do not deserve the rewards we assign to owners or managers. These ideas are often accepted by employees and empowering managers as well, and can be seen to parallel the justifications that have been cited over the years for holding onto power and controlling the behavior of others, whether it be in the workplace, in politics, or in the family.

Because of the depth and reach of this paradigm—and because, like an earlier paradigm that saw the sun as revolving around the earth—it is closely connected to our ideas about politics, religion, society, and the family. As a way of explaining why we should "thank God it's Monday," and to complete our explanation of the new paradigm, we need to search for a deeper explanation of the reasons why we should humanize the workplace.

To justify the systemic organizational changes we have discussed in earlier chapters, we need to provide an explanation for why we think the paradigm of work is shifting, and to explore the implications of this shift for the nature of work in general. We need to begin by considering the impact of humanizing work on a larger scale. We have been discussing individuals and organizations, and now need to focus on the social nature of productivity, wealth, and cooperation.

Why We Need to Humanize the Way We Work

Many of us believe the purpose of our work is to make money and accumulate wealth. In our view, however, corporations have defined wealth in a way that takes us down an empty path leading to material possessions, rather than in the direction of personal satisfaction, enjoyment, accomplishment in work, and true self-expression. We need to redefine what we think of as *wealth*.

We believe that true wealth consists not so much of the *things* we own, such as cars and computers, as in the skills, knowledge, and productive power of working individuals, as it does in the *ability to create* material wealth. If we define wealth not as a thing, but as a human activity, capacity, or potential, we see that wealth is enormously dependent on *cooperation*. Indeed, it is difficult to imagine that we could produce any of the things we consume today except through cooperation.

Take a moment to analyze your own workday. Which of your accomplishments today were solely a result of your individual efforts? Which were produced through cooperation with others? Remember that even the pencils and paper you use, the offices you occupy, the clothes you wear, and the chairs you sit on were produced by others. We are, in our view, all members of a gigantic worldwide cooperative team, and are always acting jointly and achieving our goals through cooperation, even when we are competing or working in an authoritarian environment.

Whether we work in a corporation or a nonprofit organization, in a school, hospital, farm or factory, we are able to be successful only to the extent that we cooperate with others. As our productivity has increased steadily during the 20th century, so has the scale and the need for cooperation in work. Teamwork, joint efforts, and cooperation are now necessities in the production and distribution of consumer products, in the delivery of social services, in education, and in the use of advanced technology. And cooperation is essential if productivity and accomplishment are to continue increasing. For this reason, wealth today consists primarily of people who are skilled—not simply at performing their tasks—but in using a wide variety of techniques and processes to increase their cooperation.

We have worked intensively with a number of organizations that have decided to reorganize into self-directed teams. These decisions to transform the way they work were not just whims or experiments. The viability of these companies was at stake. The ability to survive in a massively changing and fiercely competitive market depends on an organization's ability to serve its customers well, to produce higher quality products, to respond quickly to changing demand, to negotiate strong and lasting relationships, to solve problems quickly, to find and correct mistakes rapidly, and to resolve conflicts quickly and thoroughly. All of these abilities depend on cooperation among and between employees, and for most organizations today, they are life and death issues.

If we understand that our ability to work in cooperation with others is the underpinning and true basis of all our wealth, we can also see that our ability to cooperate with each other is increasingly a result of what we are calling the "humanization" of the workplace. What we are talking about is not a *thing*, but a *process*, an attitude and an intention that are given shape and form by the way we work in organizations.

One of the reasons it is so difficult to create a humanized work environment, and why we have to "justify it" in Camus's terms, is that the model we have used to design and operate our organizations is drawn from our industrial corporations, which took shape during a time of cutthroat competition and little government regulation, known as the period of the "robber barons." These powerful owners of the great railroads, steel mills, auto plants, banks, and oil companies set up their corporations as military operations in order to command and control the work process down to the smallest detail. This approach meant actively discouraging cooperation between employees, and disempowering workers, except insofar as they were cogs in a gigantic machine.

As the industrial era developed during the 20th century, the owners of these corporations became increasingly separated from the day-to-day management of their enterprises, and increasingly superfluous to decision making. The involvement of owners in the production process has decreased steadily over time as the role of managers has increased.

Today we can see a similar trend—except that it is now not merely the owners of organizations who are becoming increasingly irrelevant in day-to-day problem solving and decision making, but managers and directors as well. A large-scale historical shift appears to us to be taking place in the operation of organizations that began with all the important decisions being made exclusively by owners and directors, shifted to their being made largely by managers, and shifted again to being made by teams of self-managing employees. A parallel change has taken place in the role of managers, who began by controlling employees, then shifted to managing them, and shifted again to facilitating and encouraging their leadership.

Evolution of the Manager's Role

Every organization of any size requires a complicated coordination of specialized human skills, materials, and technology to complete its work, and the work of coordination increases with the complexity of the tasks being performed. The complexity of these skills and tasks divides the workforce into groups, for example, into sales and finance, carpenters and electricians, typists and computer programmers. Because each division, each area of specialized knowledge and skill, is distinct in how it exercises its skill, in its self-definition, its language, and its perspective on the work process, an additional branch needs to be created to regulate the whole, which comprises the "science of management."

Specialization and the division of work developed over the course of history as a result of inventions, surpluses, accumulations in production, and the concentration of people in the workplace. These changes also resulted in employees' time being freed up to develop increasingly complex skills and specialized knowledge, and to create unique consumer products. The result was that employees with general skills gradually became skilled craftsmen.

But increasing specialization also created divisions among these employees, separating them from one another, from consumers, from free time, and from liberty at work. The individual employee, for example, who once enjoyed making shoes as a work of art or craftsmanship gradually became an employee in a shoe factory with a simple, routine task related to a single part of the shoe, and now had less ability to do anything with his or her time other than make shoes. A good shoemaker might eventually become a manager of apprentice shoe makers and would have to stop making shoes; instead he or she had to make sure that the apprentices worked hard, showed up for work on time, and did not steal.

Many managers rise to their present positions by being successful craftspeople or good technicians or rapid decision makers. Often, they loved the work they did when they were in less exalted positions but cannot resist becoming managers, either for the money or the allure of power and authority. But many managers are disappointed when they find themselves far from the productive process, isolated from employees, removed from the satisfaction of accomplishing something concrete, limited in their range of activities, and separated from the creative process. Their dreams of advancement can quickly turn into nightmares.

As the level of complexity of the work process has increased, the size of the workplace has grown. Managers are now required to centralize and coordinate the work so that many different skilled employees can produce a single product, and to help the organization make a profit by requiring employees to use increasingly efficient and productive machines and work processes.

The fundamental role of the manager is to overcome these divisions in the workplace, and to link the efforts of specialized employees with different sets of skills into a single cooperative effort. Management means directing the work of others and coordinating diverse kinds of work toward the creation of a single product. The rise of management is therefore an indication both of increasing specialization and productivity, and of an increasing need for cooperation.

It is also an indication that enough profits are available to pay the salaries of a group of nonproducers, whose role is simply to coordinate the work of others. The money paid out in managers salaries can therefore be seen as income that employees might have earned if they had been allowed to manage themselves, or as money that could have been channeled back into expanded production.

Other organizational costs are attributable to management as well. Managers have contributed enormously to making our workplaces more efficient and enabling us to expand productivity beyond our wildest expectations. Yet inside many managed organizations, politics, competition, and authoritarian styles of management have produced, along with efficiency, a great deal of resentment, isolation, resistance, apathy, low morale, and inhuman treatment toward those who are managed. These "side effects" of management can be reduced, but they cannot be eliminated, other than by self-management, because there will always be a difference between following someone else's direction and finding one's own, between work that is coordinated by managers and work that is done cooperatively with one's peers, between the controllers and the controlled.

As corporations face increasing competition, as nonprofit organizations confront declining grants, as schools receive less and less funding from state and national governments, they need to learn to use scarce resources efficiently, which means that every organization has to be concerned with recapturing funds it pays to maintain top-heavy bureaucracies and vast platoons of middle managers, and with maximizing cooperation among its employees.

In the industrial model we have inherited from the robber barons, the contradictory interests and adversarial relationships between owners and managers on the one hand and employees on the other, has led to innumerable costly and time-consuming conflicts—frequently over the right to make unilateral decisions for the organization; to control how the work will be done; to announce how wages and profits will be distributed; and to discipline or discharge employees for infractions of the rules. Set against these powers of management is the practical ability of employees in self-directed teams to make the organization run, solve its problems, work efficiently, and raise morale. In the middle, in more ways than one, are the managers, trying to find some way to reconcile these conflicting forms of power over the work process.

Because the money, factories, materials, and resources used by organizations are often thought of as belonging only to its shareholders and directors, or to "the public" or "the government" in general, and not to the employees and managers who make them run, ultimate responsibility for their efficiency is seen as belonging not to everyone, but only to those at the top of the organization, while controls are placed on those at the bottom.

The primary resources that are available to managers in these organizations to encourage and motivate employees to perform their work more productively are appeals to self-interest in the form of wages and promotions or to morality and the protestant ethic or to threats of termination and discipline or to the bureaucratic enforcement of organizational rules. By contrast, in cooperatives, self-directed teams and employee-owned enterprises, employees have a direct personal, and often economic, interest in efficient self-management, which can be supplemented by appeals to self-interest or morality or lead to the creation of rules, but do not depend on them. In these employee managed organizations, encouragement and motivation are more internal than external, and therefore do not generate the same degree of resistance, apathy, cynicism, or frustration.

Work as a Source of Self-Actualization

As competition increases and funding decreases, and as the world's resources become more precious, extra efforts will be needed to reduce organizational waste. This goal can be accomplished either by downsizing and layoffs, which destroy employee, morale and ultimately reduce productivity, or by increasing morale and productivity through enhanced forms of cooperation such as teams, quality circles, and employee self-management.

The primary reason for introducing these employee participation and self-management programs, for the shareholders and directors of organizations, has not always been a humanitarian concern for the well-being of employees, but has more often been to increase profits by reducing the costs of production through expanded cooperation.

Yet the use of these techniques also reflects an increasing *obsolescence* of ownership and external managerial authority as the primary sources of organizational decision-making, and their replacement by self-managing teams of cooperating employees.

Many corporate leaders have taken the risk of sharing their power. We can point to a number of successful models, from General Motors' Saturn organization to Federal Express and Motorola, that serve as examples of winning by increasing employee cooperation. In a interview conducted recently by Warren Bennis with Jack Welsh, chairman of General Electric, Welsh enthusiastically supported employee participation and empowerment—not because it was a "fuzzy and warm thing to do" or made employees feel good, but because it was good business. Welsh maintained that unless all employees, whatever their level, role, or job, felt like they owned the whole organization, acted as responsible members of a team, and made decisions that moved the organization forward, GE could not compete successfully.

In the increasingly high-tech environment of the electronically controlled, computerized production process, the problem is no longer one of managing largely uneducated workers, but of encouraging and supporting the cooperation of highly educated employees who need leadership, not micro-management, in moving to higher levels of cooperation and productivity. All the forms of employee cooperation we have examined rely heavily on self direction, which requires a leadership that is recognized, approved, and even selected by those they lead.

These leaders are increasingly shifting decision-making authority to the level where the problems exist and where the need to solve them is the greatest—in other words, to self-managing teams for whom leadership becomes not only a means of work but also a means of self-expression. In one of our client organizations, managers who made the transition to leadership roles in a self-directed team environment reported the following results for themselves and their teams:

You're the person that leads the team. No one says they work for me, they work with me. I'm never dictatorial. We have a pretty good democracy.

I understand and am part of the day-to-day processes. If I'm a mentor and a coach, sometimes the coach goes in and plays ball. I should be aware of how the system works. I sometimes have to roll up my sleeves and help my team so that everyone is a player.

More than anything, the team leader is a facilitator. I see that everyone on the team has a role, my job is to be in tune with what the roles are. I can't do everything as well as my team members. Sometimes I need to get down and dirty and work with them in doing their job, but I'm not the expert that they are. I need to know the bare minimum of what it takes to get the job done. I need to be sure we meet the deadlines and that the quality of what we do is excellent. I also need to help everyone on the team respect each other and make sure that people understand the pressures so that they can back each other up.

I need to provide the team with a map of where we are today and where we have been and where we need to go in the reengineering process.

The role of a leader is not from the title but a status you earn and are granted by the rest of the team. Your role is to make sure it is working for the customer and keeping the team motivated and challenged.

We believe we all need meaningful work in our lives, as a way of bringing our talents, skills, and abilities to higher levels of perfection and as a way of giving something back to the people and the society we live in. How much better it must be to work with one of the manager/leaders who are quoted above, or to live in their shoes, rather than in the autocratic environments these employees were in before! They are in the process of producing a kind of personal and organizational wealth that can never be replaced—the wealth of realized human potential.

This ability to fully actualize, realize, or experience oneself as a human being through socially cooperative, self-directed work is also an increasingly important element in workplace morale, and therefore in expanded productivity. For the self-actualized employee, wealth consists more in the creative use of time than in the blind pursuit of money. A number of recent polls and academic research papers have demonstrated that employees who are given a choice between a pay raise and spending time on their own pursuits or with their children will generally choose the latter.

The quality of life outside the workplace is a major preoccupation of those in today's workforce. As masses of baby boomers reach their 50s, they are asking questions such as What's my life all about? Why am I working at a job I don't like? How can I expand my capacity for living a richer and more challenging life? In the past, these questions were asked only in private or through an underground network. Today they are coming out into the open as organizations begin to rethink their need for managerial hierarchies.

The end of the *necessity* of involuntary *work* that is managed, directed by others, and isolated, is also the beginning of the *possibility* of voluntary *labor* that is self-managed, democratically directed, and collaborative. Voluntary labor time that is self-actualizing, socially cooperative, and used to benefit society as a whole can be seen as the *human* form of wealth. The alienated, objectified wealth most of us pursue is represented only in the inadequate wages we are paid for work we do semi-voluntarily, at someone else's direction, and on someone else's behalf.

The Manager as Team Facilitator, Case #1: An Exercise

As you think about the role of managers and leaders in your organization, consider the following example, which we have taken from our experience, and ask yourself how you would respond. If you were asked to coach the manager in this situation, what advice would you give? If you were the manager, what would you have done differently?

A manager has been asked to be the facilitator of a team that is just being formed. She is very assertive, and her staff respects her highly, but rarely disagrees with her or suggests any alternatives to the ideas she puts forth. She has begun to show a sincere interest in the team process and has decided to become more involved by trying to increase the team's productivity.

At the first meeting, the other team members are quiet and uninvolved. The manager does most of the talking. Her attempts to involve other team members in the discussion are unsuccessful. Following the meeting, the manager is noticeably upset with the team's performance and the level of its involvement in the meeting and says, "Here I am giving these employees an opportunity to get involved and make serious contributions and they're not participating."

1. What recommendations would you make about how she might increase the team's participation?

_____

_____

_____

2. What would you say to help her understand her own role in the problem?

_____

_____

_____

3. What exercises or activities could you think of that might enable her to increase her self-awareness?

_____

_____

_____

4. How would you have run the meeting if you had been the manager/facilitator?

_____

_____

_____

The Power of Self-Management

Increasingly, both public and private sector organizations are searching for ways of improving their efficiency and productivity, reducing their costs, and increasing employee morale and motivation. These efforts are often called "reengineering" because they try to get at the scaffolding and basic systems of the organization. They have often failed to create a balanced organization that has one eye on the bottom line and the other on the well-being of employees, because reducing costs has come to mean layoffs and downsizing, which seriously damage morale and motivation, and because the human side of reengineering has largely been ignored.

In the search for solutions, these organizations will need to learn how to integrate cost-effective systems with humanized and cooperative work processes to make the entire effort more effective. Trying to do one or the other creates a difficult choice for management and an unsatisfactory outcome.

The term *management* has been given two alternative meanings: the first describes the frequently authoritarian decision-making power of the owners of corporations and those who act in their interests. The second refers to the team-based leadership structure that provides direction to the work process. Both types of managers engage in decision making. Both varieties of organization have systems for resolving internal conflicts, regulating production, supervising work, setting production standards, enforcing rules, and exercising responsibility for the efficient use of human and productive resources. Yet their "humanity" and their results in terms of improved employee morale and cooperation are vastly different.

The traditional method of choice for top-down managers is to make decisions. The new method is to help others learn how to make them. The old way was for managers to control the process. The new way is to develop an understanding of process and a capacity for self-control in self-managing teams. The old rule was that only shareholders or managers possessed the information. The new rule is that information is open and shared with everyone. The same points can be made, but in reverse, for employees, whose old role was to resist taking responsibility, while their new role requires taking initiative and being responsible for results.

The problem is that these new methods fly in the face of everything managers and employees have been taught, and rely on an entirely different set of skills than the ones that made them managers and employees in the first place. Several managers expressed to us their confusion with the changing demands on their role, while others indicated their excitement at the opportunities:

> *Hey, this was a tough transition for me. But it works; I like the role of player coach instead of dominant owner.*
>
> *I'm confused by the word empowerment. I'm not empowered to say to my team members we will do this my way. My team members are more empowered than I am as a team leader.*

I'm attracted by the entrepreneurial aspects of the job. The role is not defined, so I can create it as I go. It is exciting to be the first department to change—we are on the ground floor of a changing environment.

I can be a valuable resource to my client organization and the company as a whole. We are not just here to gather revenue but to provide information in a format that can be used by sales to help make decisions and react in a more profitable way.

There is a natural resistance to innovation and change, not only because they make outmoded practices obsolete, but also because they call into question the life choices and commitments of the individuals who were schooled in these practices. Organizational transformation is even more difficult because of the natural resistance of bureaucracies to change and the slowness of collective decision making. While we see many of the organizational changes we have been describing increasing in pace and complexity, we also see them generating consequences that often go unexamined.

An example of a change that has consequences in the way we work is strategic planning. To complete any complex organizational change today requires a strategic planning process that works smoothly. Strategic planning requires an honest and realistic assessment of what is not working. Developing a vision; agreeing on a set of achievable goals; identifying the barriers to achieving them; agreeing on a unified strategy; preparing an action plan; achieving consensus on the assignment of roles and tasks; establishing a system to monitor progress, evaluate, and self-correct; and acknowledging and celebrating successes can all be seen as traditional management functions, yet none can be accomplished today without the leadership, teamwork, and cooperation of everyone in the workplace.

In humanistic organizations, it is no longer possible for owners or managers acting alone to engage in effective strategic planning or successfully impose broad organizational changes. If they do not secure the active and voluntary participation of employees, the change will fall short. Moreover, where employees are given greater decision-making authority, the primary methods for accomplishing organizational change shift from orders, coercion, threats, unilateral efforts, and decision by fiat to leadership, education, dialogue, negotiation, conflict resolution, and consensus. The managers of change in humanistic organizations need to be leaders more than managers, and facilitators or educators more than decision makers.

Increased efficiency without self-management means increased profits in the short run, but competition, resistance, and an antagonistic relationship with employees in the long-run. At maximum efficiency, all employees in a humanistic organization understand that they bear both individual and collective responsibility for the entire effort and are thereby entitled to participate equally in its rewards. The greater the involvement in responsibility and decision-making, the greater the understanding that inefficient production harms everyone, and the greater the need to allow people to share in the benefits that flow from taking on that extra responsibility.

A primary task of humanistic management is therefore to search for ways of transferring as many managerial tasks as possible to employees, in an effort to reduce the level of unproductive employment and find ways of sharing all the decisions the organization needs to make. This transition requires employees at every level to become leaders, and to learn effective communication, group process, collaborative problem solving, nonadversarial forms of negotiation, and conflict resolution skills so they can become self-conscious organizers of their own continuous personal and organizational transformation.

A central purpose of humanized, self-managing organizations should therefore be to broaden employee leadership and participation in decision making wherever possible. In the same way that political education empowers all citizens to become leaders, increases participation in political discourse, and seeks to expand the base of political decision making as broadly as possible, management education should be aimed at increasing the ranks of competent leaders and self-managers from among the ranks of employees.

The Manager as Team Player, Case #2: An Exercise

As an individual or with your team, consider the following case drawn from one of our clients. How would you solve it in a new context as you rethink the roles of leaders and managers? Imagine you are the facilitator of an interdepartmental, multilevel team working on a new quality-improvement project on a cross-departmental basis. The team has been meeting for eight months and has reviewed all of its processes and developed a plan to implement quality improvement.

Though all team members agreed to the plan, they have different levels of commitment to implementing it. The team member who is least committed to the plan is a manager who represents one of the functions that plays a significant part in the implementation process. This particular manager is the only member representing that function on the team.

The next step is for the team to begin implementation through a pilot project. However, for the last two meetings, the team has not been able to reach consensus on how to implement the pilot program. This impass is attributed to the manager's schedule and his doubts about the proposed options.

1. What actions would you take as the facilitator/coach?

    _____

    _____

    _____

2. How would you redefine the managers role?

    _____

    _____

    _____

3. What is the team's responsibility to move the consensus decision-making process toward implementation?

    _____

    _____

    _____

4. How would you coach the manager?

    _____

    _____

    _____

5. What kind of intervention would you make with the team as a whole?

    _____

    _____

    _____

An Example of Humanizing the Workplace— A Different Approach to Absenteeism

Absenteeism and laziness among employees is an enormous problem in most workplaces. The usual solutions to this problem are to counsel the employee regarding the rules and then begin a process of progressive discipline that proceeds from oral warning to written reprimand to suspension and termination. Let's consider, however, how a humanized organization might approach this problem and use different methods to produce very different results.

Before we begin looking for alternative solutions, let's try to understand more about what the problem actually is, and why the employee does not show up or engage actively in her work. One possible reason is that, at a given hourly wage, the greater the absenteeism, tardiness, or sloth on the part of the employee, the higher the actual rate of pay. If an employee is paid the same amount but works fewer hours, she has, by nonperformance, voted herself a pay raise! If she earns $10.00 an hour but only works a half hour for that pay, she has just doubled her salary.

Another reason for absenteeism and laziness might be that the organization's rules were, in all probability, not created, monitored, or enforced by employees, but by people who are paid a salary without having to clock in a specific number of hours each week. In this way, absent or lazy employees are able to see themselves as doing exactly the same thing as their absent owners, unproductive managers, and other "lazy" workers, whose salaries also drain the organization's profits. Such behavior results in less money for wage increases, productive reinvestment, or expanded social wealth to employees who care about doing their jobs right. The absent or lazy employee can look around and say, "I'm just taking time for my own needs, just like the boss does when he goes to the golf course or my manager does when she takes time off to run personal errands, or when we sit in useless meetings where nothing gets done anyway."

Absenteeism, tardiness, and laziness among employees can thus be seen as the flip side of the owner's luxury or the manager's time off. The individual employee who is absent or tardy also wants to enjoy free time and satisfy his or her personal needs; she takes small-scale liberties to gain a share of the apparent surplus of available time. Yet all these activities are subtractions from the organization's productivity, and when they are available only to some, they represent a selfishness that is shortsighted because it does not recognize the interdependent, cooperative nature of work or the stake everyone has in the work of the whole.

Lost work time due to tardiness and absenteeism is a problem common to all but the most spirited and humanistic organizations, partly because people have many good and important reasons for missing work. Nevertheless, production suffers even in enlightened organizations when crucial workers are late or absent without notice, regardless of the method or system of work in which it occurs.

The focus in most organizations is on the discipline and eventual termination of the absent or lazy employee as the only way of solving this problem. Little is done to search for collaborative solutions, and the result is to remove the individual and do nothing to solve the systemic issues of employee motivation. With adequate notice and advance preparation, replacements can usually be found to fill in. If not, training replacements, dividing the work into parts that can be performed more simply, assigning work to machines, and similar methods may reduce the long-term level of loss, but none of these measures solve the problem.

Providing assistance to employees in meeting their personal needs may help resolve the problems faced by a particular employee. For example, if an employee is having marital problems, marriage counseling may be helpful. A program of "positive discipline" and a set of negotiated and agreed-upon objectives may also be beneficial, regardless of the type of organization or the context or paradigm it is operating under.

The root causes of absenteeism, laziness, and other behavioral problems, however, are often ignored or papered over in the assumption that nothing can be done to resolve them short of termination. Unresolved, they are allowed to fester or find outlets in resistance, inefficiency, apathy, sullenness, sabotage, and resentment. Where employees are trained in facilitation, communication, problem solving, conflict resolution, counseling, coaching, mediation, and similar skills, these problems are considerably reduced, and cooperation is used to substantially improve employee performance.

Here are a number of alternative approaches to the problem that are more participative and democratic:

1. Begin by asking employees to identify the rules they need to agree on in order to be more productive, and to affirm these rules by consensus. No group of employees will create such a set of rules without addressing the issues of laziness and absenteeism, which

will make the rules theirs, rather than someone else's, thereby making enforcement everyone's responsibility.

2. Allow employees to monitor and enforce the system themselves and support efforts to do so proactively and preventatively. This approach will make managers seem less like police or truant officers and create a sense of fairness about the process.

3. Create an early-warning system to identify potential employee problems before they get out-of-hand. Absenteeism usually begins with slack morale, which will be noticed by co-workers long before it is picked up by a manager.

4. Encourage team members to discuss the problem among themselves and to use brainstorming techniques to search for possible solutions. This approach will encourage the team to take responsibility for the success of these techniques in solving the problem.

5. Encourage an honest self-evaluation by the employee and elicit his or her suggestions about possible solutions. This can be done much more readily by a team of one's peers than by a manager, and the chances are good that the employee already knows what the best solution would be.

6. Look closely, openly and honestly at whatever the actual problem is and engage the team in efforts at cooperative problem solving. Perhaps the problem is an unresolved conflict between co-workers or employees who feel they have been passed over for promotion, in which case, mediation or a training program might become solutions.

7. Create incentives and rewards, either moral or material, for changed behavior and allow these to be suggested by employees as a whole or by the employee who is creating the problem. Build compensation systems as a reward for extra effort. In one organization we worked with, every team member's salary depended on their evaluations by the entire team, by other teams, and by their customer.

8. Offer additional training in team process, communicate more clearly the costs of absenteeism, and encourage the team to demonstrate that the employee's failure to work means more work for his or her fellow team members.

9. Encourage a peer coaching or peer counseling process, in which employees are trained to be coaches and counselors to one another. Co-workers can be quite effective as peer coaches or counselors and may see things the manager misses or cannot bring up in the absence of clear evidence, such as problems with alcoholism or drug addiction. One organization we worked with titled these coaches "resource managers" because it believed the employee was a valuable resource to the whole organization.

10. Make a referral to an outside resource, such as an employee-assistance program. A successful referral system depends on an accurate method of assessing what the real problem is, and any assessment by a manager will be less accurate than one made by co-workers who work alongside the employee.

11. Mediate the dispute, using a peer-based conflict resolution process, or an outside mediator if needed. Peer mediation is a highly effective method for resolving deeper levels of conflict because it is based in consensus and focused on the future rather than the past.

12. If none of these methods prove effective, return to the team and allow it to decide whether to discipline, transfer, or fire the employee, and begin the steps involved in progressive discipline, leading to final and binding arbitration.

In order to change the employee's attitude, which is often the real problem, the team will need to clearly communicate to its lazy or absentee member that it is not the faceless CEO or autocratic manager who is being ripped off by her behavior, but her team members, and ultimately herself.

The absent employee will eventually need to realize that although she may be able to temporarily increase her rate of pay by being absent or lazy, other team members wages are being reduced to the same degree. If the organization's purpose suffers, so will the ability of the employee to benefit in the long run, or to be proud of his contribution, and the "self" that such an employee creates through her work will be one she will have to admit she does not like.

The gradual elimination of absenteeism, tardiness, laziness, and similar problems in self-directed teams thus reflects the growing consciousness of individual employees that they are members of a cooperative community of self-actualizing producers with the power to affect their own lives, as well as the lives of others, and the ability to participate in the rewards that flow from their cooperation.

Creating Solutions to Behavioral Problems: An Exercise

As you consider the alternative solutions to absenteeism we outlined above, project them into your own work environment. Select a problem you would like to address in your organization. As an individual or with a partner or team members, plan a way to begin the problem-solving process by answering the following questions:

1. What behavioral problem do you want to address?

_____

_____

_____

2. Who will you need to involve in order to solve the problem?

_____

_____

_____

3. What steps, similar to those listed above, will you take to begin the process?

_____

_____

_____

4. What backup plans or alternative solutions will you try if those fail?

_____

_____

_____

5. How will you measure the results?

_____

_____

_____

6. How will you obtain the cooperation of the problem employee in solving the problem?

_____

_____

_____

7. What will you do to encourage and reward improvement?

_____

_____

_____

8. How will you involve the employee's peers, co-workers, and team members?

_____

_____

_____

We all know from personal experience that our ability to recognize that we are responsible for our own improvement is far stronger when it is based on self-discipline, or when it comes from feedback from our peers, than when it emanates from criticism directed at us by our supervisors, and when our problems are discussed in a positive way, rather than delivered to us disrespectfully, or as judgments masquerading as evaluation.

Employees can be helped to understand and correct their mistakes far more effectively by their co-workers without being coerced or threatened with discipline or termination. They can work with their problems over a period of time to learn from them and improve their skills. Positive discipline techniques acknowledge effort as well as performance, and treat employees as adults who are able to grow, learn, and listen to feedback that is future oriented and nonpunitive.

The point can be made more fundamentally. The behavioral and economic problems of many of today's organizations, their notorious inefficiencies, their chronic conflicts and poor morale, their centralization at the expense of democracy, and their often shoddy service and bureaucratic sluggishness, are aggravated by authoritarian discipline that is imposed from above and ameliorated by humanistic leadership exercised from below.

Responding to Absenteeism, Case #3: An Exercise

A case example drawn from our work with teams reveals how absenteeism impacts everyone, often beyond the individuals who are causing the problem. Assume you are the leader of an eight-member team. The team has been meeting for several months. Although the team has made progress, attendance has been uneven. One of the team members has only attended half the scheduled meetings. In addition, this individual has not participated in any of the team's planning or brainstorming sessions. The lack of attendance was rationalized by the team member on the ground that the meeting was not important to completing the team's project. The member felt his job responsibilities should take priority over team activities. You are also aware of the following additional information:

A. The team member does not like team meetings and generally tends to perform independently in a specialist position.

B. Team members are beginning to notice and comment on the team member's uneven attendance.

I. What actions would you take to improve the team member's attendance and involvement?

_____

_____

_____

2. How would you respond to the absenteeism in your interactions with the individual?

_____

_____

_____

3. What would you say to other members of the team? At team meetings?

_____

_____

_____

4. What would you do to encourage honest feedback and self-evaluation without triggering defensiveness?

_____

_____

_____

Humanization as a Motivational Technique

In a recent workshop, we asked participants to identify the questions with which they were struggling in their roles as leaders of change. We received the following questions from a number of managers in a variety of organizations that included a health care insurance provider, an auto manufacturer, a banker, and a software developer. They wanted to know:

How do you truly empower employees without losing clear, overall, direction, goals, standards, etc.?

How do you inoculate new employees against being poisoned by enemies of change within the organization? (The gossip and cynicism of the "bad apples" often undermines good people on the way in the door.)

How do you generate trust and hope in the face of uncertainty, downsizing, and massive change?

How do you encourage staff to develop and emerge as leaders in a self-directed management division surrounded by a stress-filled environment?

In the past, managers have used two methods to improve the motivation of employees and to answer the difficult questions posed above. At the positive end, they have given out rewards or incentives, and at the negative end, punishments or disincentives. The former often induce greed, while the latter generate fear. The former rely on the carrot, the latter rely on the stick. Yet motivation is merely an answer to the question "why," when asked in relation to a particular action. The answers often vary from desire to greed to fear, and to confuse their answers even further, individuals often have false perceptions about their real motivations.

Yet there is a third alternative. Both greed and fear, as motivational methods, are *external* to the employee. Teams, collaborative process, and humanized workplaces encourage employees to develop *internal* sources of motivation that are far more powerful than any that could be established externally. Work, under these conditions, has the capacity of becoming a labor of love, and when that happens, the separation between work and leisure begins to disappear. Work for others is done grudgingly, while work for one's self or one's team members is often done with joy.

"Give us your unsolvable problems." This challenging request came from a team of engineers, computer system analysts, and embracers of change who formed themselves into a team in a large telecommunications company for the purpose of taking on the toughest problem faced by the organization. Ted, the team leader, told us the following story. One of the switching mechanisms that was responsible for kicking in when a large telephone system went down took from five to seven hours to switch over to a new cable pathway. This switching time was unacceptable to their biggest clients, but no one could find a solution. Ted decided that the only way to solve the problem was to turn it over to a highly motivated team—to find a new way by stepping outside of the old contexts, paradigms, behaviors, and usual patterns of problem solving.

Ted's team was willing to use the "trash can" approach we described in the introduction. They threw out all the old ways of working. Ted told his crew he would be responsible for any of their failures, and they would be protected, so they could take whatever risks they wanted and experiment freely because their jobs were safe. The team members gave themselves an impossible deadline of six months to come up with a solution. They began with a quick and dirty operation to meet growing client pressure for a better response. In the space of four months they had achieved their goal. They successfully brought the switching time down to less than 10 minutes!

They had so much fun creating this powerful team, they renamed themselves the "Impossible Projects" team and asked the organization to give them all their toughest nuts to crack, all the problems that had no solutions, all the difficulties everyone else had given up on. They were motivated by the excitement of having accomplished the impossible, and of doing so in concert, as part of a united cooperative effort. The company agreed, and the team continues having fun, working fast, and producing incredible results by taking risks and embracing change.

If an average employee were asked why he or she is working, the largest percentage of answers would be "in order to eat" or "to buy the things I need or want." Work is seen as instrumental to the satisfaction of other needs, rather than as a *need in itself.* Yet we know that the satisfaction of physical needs and wants does not eliminate the need for meaningful work, since we use activity to define and shape ourselves. Ted's team was able to achieve something far more important than income, not only for the organization and its customers, but also for themselves as individuals and as members of the team. They were able to reach beyond their known abilities, and in the process redefined who they were.

If anything, team members who work alongside each other are more truly self-realized than those who work in isolation and miss the enormous satisfaction that comes from meeting challenges and contributing to others. The motivation to work with others who are equally empowered is vastly different from the motivation to work for someone who is not empowering you.

If we look at the process we are describing from a different direction, we are talking about democracy in work. The logic of democracy is that everyone participates in making the decisions that affect their lives, that all contributions are valuable and everyone is equally entitled to be heard, that diversity of perspective makes us stronger, and that the product of the whole working together is greater than the sum of its individual parts.

On a broader level, without democracy in the workplace there can be no effective system of political or social democracy. Without political and social democracy there can be no effective democracy in the workplace. Undemocratic management in the workplace and undemocratic processes in government and society are mutually reinforcing, and lead to a culture of secrecy, corruption, inefficiency, selfishness, and a self-expanding inflexible bureaucracy.

For industrial democracy to succeed, we need to move from hierarchy and centralism to democracy and self-management, from control by managerial coercion to self-control through collaboration and consensus. As the externally imposed values of management become democratic and are internalized, we have found that the need for bureaucracy and excessive regulation begins to disappear.

Improving productivity through employee participation and self-managing teams is therefore a part of the *liberation* of individuals from selfishness, from alienation, from the resistance that results from "inhuman" treatment, and from economic and social disempowerment. This transformation cannot be accomplished by any externally imposed rules, but only by all employees acting together as owners, and ultimately by actually owning their organizations, that is, by making socially and organizationally conscious choices, and by learning through training and the accumulation of experience how to make these choices in the interests of the whole. In humanized workplaces, responsibility becomes general so that ownership begins to lose its meaning and the management of work becomes social and cooperative, and much more fun.

Many people believe that individual success and team advancement are necessarily in conflict and that we must chose between them, but our experience and examples show that self-actualization, or *individual* liberty, and cooperative planning, or *social* liberty, are not inherently antagonistic, but potentially synergistic. While there have certainly been times in the workplace when individual liberty has been restricted in order to expand social liberty and vice versa, it is becoming increasingly clear that neither can expand beyond the limit created by a lack of expansion in the other. At the point of their interconnection, the free social individual becomes a self-conscious and empowered cooperative producer, and the apparent contradiction between individual and social liberty is broken.

With genuine empowerment, every individual and team inside an organization benefits *directly* by increasing the productivity of every other individual and team along with their own, and consequently, all are able to benefit by cooperation in developing more efficient techniques that advance, rather than retard, the productive process. Enormous improvements in organizational performance will become possible when we humanize our workplaces, because the creativity, independence, cooperation, and high morale that are characteristic of self-directed teams enable them to collaborate and plan ways of expanding the productive process far beyond what was possible under the old contexts and paradigms. Only by humanizing the workplace will this expansion in productivity, and in free time as the human form of wealth, become possible.

Conclusion

We have tried in this book to combine our practical experiences with thoughts and ideas about the emerging paradigm of the humanized workplace. We hope it has made you think and encouraged you to act a little differently in your own workplace, and perhaps feel more entitled to participate in changing it to reflect your own needs and desires. We hope you will join the current movements that are bringing human qualities to organizations on a day-to-day basis—one organization, one workplace, one person at a time.

In ending, we want to leave you with the following thoughts reportedly expressed by Joan of Arc on hearing herself sentenced to be burned at the stake. They express our belief in the importance of living our lives, especially at work, in full knowledge that what we believe, and how we live in support of our beliefs, matters. It may help you choose to live your own work life more humanely and participate in your workplace as though your life depends on it. It does.

> *I know this now.*
> *Every man gives his life for what he believes.*
> *Every woman gives her life for what she believes.*
> *Sometimes people believe in little or nothing,*
> *yet they give their lives to that little or nothing.*
> *One life is all we have and we live it*
> *as we believe in living it. And then it is gone.*
> *But to sacrifice what you are and live without belief,*
> *that's more terrible than dying.*

INDEX

Printed in the United States
3542

9 780786 310968